A WORD OF CAUTION FROM BERNICE

I've been married to Red Green for 30 years and...
30 years? My God, has it been that long?...
Sorry. Where was I? Oh, yes.

STOP

Do not under any circumstances

attempt to use any of the suggestions or make any
of the projects or listen to any of the advice of
anybody in this book except mine. If possible,
don't even read the book yourself. Just buy it and
burn it, and take pleasure in knowing that you've
helped the world by preventing at least one copy
from getting into the wrong hands.

On behalf of wives and mothers and ambulance drivers
everywhere, don't do this stuff. Like most men, my husband
deteriorates with encouragement.

RED GREEN TALKS CARS

A LOVE STORY

Steve Smith
Rick Green

Additional material by
Peter Wildman

Illustrations by
The Artist Formerly Known as Rick

Prima Publishing

PRIMA PUBLISHING and colophon are registered trademarks of Prima Communications, Inc.

Library of Congress cataloging-in-publication data on file
ISBN: 0-7615-1112-1

97 98 99 00 01 HH 10 9 8 7 6 5 4 3 2
Printed in the United States of America

How to Order

Single copies may be ordered from Prima Publishing, P.O. Box 1260BK, Rocklin, CA 95677; telephone (916) 632-4400. Quantity discounts are also available. On your letterhead, include information concerning the intended use of the books and the number of books you wish to purchase.

Visit us online at http://www.primapublishing.com

DEDICATION

This is dedicated to the brave men and women who have leaned over and lain under their cars at three o'clock in the morning. Somewhere in Heaven, there's a parking spot with your name on it. It's around the back, by the dumpster.

FORWARD

Signified by the letter D, found between Reverse, Neutral
and Low, and a better life choice than any of the alternatives,
with the exception of Park.

INTRODUCTION

Having already written one book, this is now my other book.

This is a book for anybody who loves cars or likes cars or is ambivalent towards cars or dislikes cars or hates cars. For anyone who has ever owned, rented, borrowed, stolen, ridden in, or looked at a car. There is not a lot of worthwhile advice in this book, but I'm guessing that's not a complete surprise to you.

I hope you enjoy this book but, having already cashed the cheque, I'm not all that concerned.

Red Green

NO DIRECTIONS

I need to talk to all of you ladies out there to help you understand why us men do the things we do. For example, the way we won't stop and ask for directions when we're lost.

Okay, it all comes down to pride. We're out there driving around in our own vehicle, burning gas, wearing sunglasses, looking good. People who see us driving by would never guess that we have no idea where we are. And we don't want to tell them. Men don't enjoy the thought of going up to total strangers and saying, "You may not know this, but I'm a moron." In contrast, the woman we're travelling with is often very anxious to share this knowledge with the world. It somehow eases her burden.

To a woman, getting lost on a trip is a blameless act of nature— to a man, it's a personal failure. He knew where he was when he left home—he doesn't know where he is now. Somewhere along the way he crossed the line between the world he knows and the world he doesn't know. To a man, this is how he felt when he got married or had kids. If he admits he's lost in the car, he'll have to admit that he's lost everywhere and that's way too much to ask. So just bite your tongue and let him circle the block a few more times.

Men aren't lost, they just go the long way.

A Man and His Car

She was a 1952 Pontiac coupe with a flathead six and the torpedo back. My brother and I did a valve job on her in the driveway (which was just two dirt ruts in the lawn and a lot of oil stains). The job took us all weekend, including the four hours he spent lying on the grass groaning after getting nailed in the groin with a spring compressor. (That may explain how a brother of mine could father a son like Harold.)

We got that greasy monster back together and had enough parts left over to make a roof rack. The engine eventually ran, but the block was cracked so the water would seep in through the cylinder wall and sit on top of one of the pistons. Antifreeze destroys cylinders, so we didn't use any. Every winter night the water on the piston would freeze into a hockey puck of ice and, when we started the car on the other five cylinders, the piston would smash the puck into the head, close the spark plug gap and short out the ignition coil.

The motor mounts on the right side were broken so every time we popped the clutch, the engine would jerk over on its left side, pulling the gas pedal to the floor. She had a six-volt battery and vacuum wipers, two features that pretty much guaranteed we couldn't see where we were going and nobody could see us coming. The cigarette lighter was a pack of matches, the ashtray was the window. We didn't smoke, but the car did.

The tires were so old they were bald, and we were so young, we weren't. One was a white wall, and we were saving for more, till my brother found some old house paint.

We did all the repairs ourselves, which is why the right rear window was plywood, the muffler clamps were coat hangers, the hood latch was a coat hanger, the radio antenna was a coat hanger (no wonder our clothes were lying on the floor), and the door handles were a pair of vice-grips. We got in her by climbing through the open window. The rust hole on the fender was a perfect step up, but climbing out would've ruined our tuxedos on prom night. Luckily, we didn't go.

The radio was all tubes and we had to turn it on an hour before we left if we were hoping for music before we got to school. The doors rattled and the windows shook, and the heater was designed for a much warmer climate. The car broke down every time we went out in it. Telling somebody we were going to be at a certain place at a certain time was like calling ourselves millionaires just because we'd bought a lottery ticket. It was barely roadworthy when we got it, and it went downhill from there. It was a worthless piece of crap.

Man, we loved that car.

We went to football games and parties and on dates and down to the beach. Sometimes it would start when we didn't expect it to and we'd go for a drive just so we didn't waste an opportunity. It had bench seats front and back so you could really cuddle up. Or do those C.O.D. turns, which meant Come Over Darling—one hard right turn and she slid across the shiny naugahyde and into your arms. And you knew the girl liked you the minute she got in that car, because it meant she trusted you more than her own eyes.

No seatbelts because in those days cars were a lot more dangerous when they were parked than when they were moving. It was a simpler time then. Luckily we were simpler too, so we fit right in. People expected us to be late or maybe not even show up. We didn't have a huge load of expectation placed on our vehicle or ourselves. They gave us leeway in those days.

Guys like us needed leeway.

driving song #71

Tailgatin'

On a warm summer's day when we're
    not after bass,
We get out the van and fill her up
    with gas.
Get behind a car driving down the
    road,
Then we move up so darn close it
    looks like we're being towed.
Tailgatin', Tailgatin',
Kinda looks like the vehicles are
    matin'
Tailgatin', Tailgatin',
Just make sure your brakes are
    okay...
In retrospect that was an
    oversight on our part

WHAT TO DO WHEN YOUR CAR WON'T START

You don't have to be a licenced mechanic to have a car that won't start. Here are some simple steps that will save you money by preventing you from going to the mall.

STEP ONE: IGNITION CHECK

- Is the key in the ignition?
- Is it the car key?
- Are you turning it the right way?
- Does the motor turn over?
- Do you know what "turn over" means? (You married guys do.)
- If the motor doesn't turn over, check the battery. Wipe off the top of the battery and lay your tongue across both terminals. Check your watch. If you blacked out for over an hour, the battery is fine.
- Remove a spark plug for a random test. Slide your ear lobe into the spark plug gap and have a friend crank the starter. If it works, you should now have a pierced ear.

When you're satisfied that the ignition is okay, move on to the fuel check.

STEP TWO: FUEL CHECK

- Does the fuel gauge show gas?
- Does the fuel gauge work?
- Is there a fuel gauge?
- Have you ever looked at the fuel gauge before?
- Did your teenager borrow the vehicle and promise, swear and vow on his honour to remember to gas it up?
- Remove the gas cap, do you see gas?
- Do you smell gas?
- Do you taste gas?
- Are you standing in gas?
- If you enjoy travelling, hold a match up to the gas filler tube.
- Disconnect the outlet tube from the fuel pump. It's probably a metric fitting so you might as well snip her off with side cutters. Look down the end of the tube while a friend cranks the motor

over. If you detect a fair amount of excess gas in your eye, the fuel pump is fine. Re-connect the tube with duct tape.

- Find every adjusting screw on the carburetor and turn them all the way one way. Try the engine. Now turn them all the way the other way. Try the engine again. Now set them all roughly somewhere in the middle.

- The automatic choke mechanism can rarely be fixed so whack it a few times with a hammer just for fun.

Now that you've ruled out ignition or fuel problems, move on to alternate starting techniques.

STEP THREE: ALTERNATE STARTING TECHNIQUES

- For an older car that has never had a tune-up or an oil change or a tank of brand-name gas, the car battery may not have enough power. Attach battery cables to the terminals. Run the cables into the house and plug them into the stove circuit. Set your rad to 425 degrees and your engine should be done in about an hour. Baste lightly, serves six anxious passengers.

- Maybe the starting motor doesn't turn the engine over fast enough. Take your car to the top of a big hill, or better still always remember to park at the top of a big hill, then turn on the ignition and roll it down. Pop the clutch often and with attitude. If the car won't start, try rolling it backwards down the hill. If that doesn't work, try rolling it sideways into a ravine.

- Bring a crushed car home from the auto wrecker. Park it in front of your car and say, "This could be you." If a car won't start with threats, it's finished. But you still deserve some satisfaction.

STEP FOUR: SATISFACTION

A Saturday afternoon with a ten-pound sledge hammer can really ease the frustration of a car that refuses to start. And when you've had your fill from every conceivable angle, hose it down with barbecue starter and give it a Viking funeral. A stunning milestone in the battle of Man against Machine.

STEP FIVE: AFTERTHOUGHT

Make sure it's your car.

THE CAR BUFFS ABOUT BAD DRIVING

HAROLD ASKS:

HAROLD

Our Car Buffs today are my Uncle Red and his best friend, Dougie Franklin. We've received a letter that reads
> *"Dear Car Buffs, I consider myself to be an above average driver. However the judge who took my licence away suggested I may not be as good as I think. Exactly how do you tell if you're a bad driver?"*

RED

Well, Dougie, bad driving is certainly your area of expertise.

DOUGIE

No kidding, Red. You want to know about bad drivers, I'm your man. I must run into one of those bad drivers every month or so. Usually head-on. Okay, first of all, I blame our driver education system.

RED

Yep. You're right there. I agree.

DOUGIE

I mean a kid spends four years at school learning how to control a pencil, which has no moving parts, could never go more than about a mile an hour, and won't burst into flame if you roll it over. Then they spend a few weeks learning to drive a two-ton ball of metal, glass and rubber, which goes a hundred and fifty clicks an hour down the highway.

RED

A hundred and fifty?

DOUGIE

And them driving instructors spend hours teaching kids how to parallel park, and basically no time on stuff like avoiding high-speed collisions. How much danger can there be while you're parallel parking?

RED

Well, Dougie, remember that time you parallel parked into the tanker truck and...

DOUGIE

That was a freak accident, Red. My point is that there's all this time on parking and nothing on high-speed collisions. And speaking for myself, I parallel park maybe once a month, whereas I'm always avoiding high-speed collisions.

RED

Not always, Dougie. Remember that load of cabbages...

DOUGIE

That was a freak accident, Red. The fact remains that we're not teaching kids right. And how can we? The teachers are talking theory. You've gotta learn from someone who's been there. Like my own family. We've had every kind of automobile accident there is. Sideswipe, roll over, head-on, rear ender, T-bone. We're the ones who should be teaching the kids. You get me, my dad and my brother in front of a classroom and I guarantee ya it'd bring down the number of bad drivers on the road.

RED

Yeah. By three.

QUICK Driving Tip

When colliding with a tree, try to smack it above the first branch where the trunk is weaker and a bird's nest may absorb some of the impact.

A DOZEN EXCUSES TO GIVE THE COPS

Cops pulled you over? Clip this list of excuses and tape it to your visor and talk your way out of a ticket.

1. I was speeding so I could get home before you set up this radar trap.

2. I was speeding so I could get out of the way so you could aim your radar at the guy behind me who was really going fast.

3. Yes, I was speeding towards you. You looked like you needed help.

4. I was speeding to beat the sunset. Both of my headlights are burned out.

5. But Officer, how can I signal my turns if my turn indicators haven't worked since I ran into that police car five months ago? I mean, let's be fair.

6. I'm the regional quality control officer for the Acme Radar Gun Company and I'm here doing a spot check of our product. It seems to be functioning perfectly, so my work here is done. Goodbye.

7. I tried to stop in time, but the guy ahead of me was leading too close.

8. He was driving in my blind spot, and his horn was in my deaf spot.

9. The other driver failed to acknowledge my lack of control.

10. The other driver failed to acknowledge the possibility that I might run the Stop sign.

11. The pedestrian was taking up the whole sidewalk and left me no room.

12. The other vehicle was a hazard because it was driving at the speed limit.

A DOZEN EXCUSES TO GIVE THE JUDGE

So the police didn't believe your excuses? Well, clip this list, and put it in the pocket of your best outfit, because that's what you'll wear for your court appearance.

1. Your honour, I would have come to a complete stop, but I wanted to get out of the way of the police car that was following me.

2   I didn't need to use my signals. I turn at that corner every day.

3. Tailgating? I was trying to give him a push, but he was going too fast. Boy, you try to be helpful.

4. I speed because it wastes gas and sends a message to certain Middle East powers that this great country won't be held hostage to oil interests and threats of embargo. It's basically a political act and I'm a political prisoner.

5. Your honourableness, my radio is stuck at full volume on an all-polka station. I had to drive fast. My non-violent side was running out of time.

6. Your honourary, I wasn't speeding? The radar just bounced off the metal plate in my head as it bobbed to the beat of my Bobby Vinton 8-track.

7. Your holiness, the earth orbits the sun at 243,000 kilometres per hour. Compared to that I wasn't speeding at all.

8. Your honorarium, I saw the sign 401, and thought it was the speed limit, not the highway number.

9. Your honorific, society is to blame for giving me the driver's licence. I'm merely a victim of incompetent examiners.

10. I wasn't wearing a seatbelt because I knew the cops would make me get out the car. They always do.

11. Yes, I was swerving down the highway, but it's not easy to kill a mosquito with a coffee cup at 80 miles an hour.

12. I would never have been driving that recklessly if the police hadn't been chasing me.

auto BIOGRAPHY
- ARNIE DOGAN

RED

Welcome to Auto-Biography, where members of Possum Lodge share remembrances of cars past. Arnie Dogan of Dogan and Sons Roofing is here. Arnie, do you remember your very first car?

ARNIE

A Volvo. A '74. Very safe. Built like a tank. And perfect for the roofing business. You could get ten cases of shingles in the trunk.

HAROLD

I got a case of shingles in a hot tub once.

RED

I would have thought you'd drive something a little sportier, Arnie.

ARNIE

No, Red. When you fall off a roof three or four times a day, you're not really looking for excitement. I never worried about getting hurt in my Volvo. Although one time when I was getting out of it, Dad dropped a ladder on me. The car was fine.

RED

I'll bet our readers would like to know what a teenager did in a Volvo, besides drive to the emergency ward.

ARNIE

A lot of dates, Red. Lot of dates.

RED

Oh yeah?

ARNIE

Yeah, they'd carry my crutches and change my bandages. And on a clear night we'd cruise up to Rock Reef Point and just gaze out over the rooftops and try to spot where Dad and I had left the ladder. I wrote a country song about that car...

It was made of steel and Naugahyde
    With five wheels, counting the spare
You never knew where you were going
But you were pretty sure you'd be able
    to thumb a ride back.

I remember the night of the accident
All that was left was the radio aerial
The doctors couldn't remove it
So now I walk with a limp, but I get over
    200 stations.

Possum Lodge Traffic Bylaws:

#1. No Parking on the Grass.
    No Parking on the Beach.
    No Parking in the Lodge.
    No Parking in the Lake.
    Please practice parallel
    parking. Not triangular
    parking, tetrahedral
    parking, rhombus parking,
    or stacking cars on top
    of each other.

        Obey these Bylaws—
    or face my frown. I'M SERIOUS!

        Officer Noel Christmas

RUSTPROOFING YOUR CAR

In the winter the government dumps so much salt on the roads your car turns into a bag of chips. Rust chips. And come spring, when the chips are down, you'll be sittin' there with a bare chassis which is not only embarrassing, it's against the law.

Now the normal solution is to cover the rust with fibreglass but there's a lot of work and expertise involved with that and that puts it outside of our capabilities.

MOOSE'S CEMENT CAR

Moose Thompson went another way. He covered his whole car with an inch and a half of concrete which gave it an interesting look. It really cut down on his gas mileage, but if he's ever in an accident, he wins.

But I like to take a fresh approach to the problem of resurfacing your automobile. I'd like you to think about linoleum. It's strong, it's durable, lightweight, and if you ever get into a fender bender, a good quality cushion floor could save your life. And it's easy as heck to install using the Handyman's Secret Weapon—duct tape.

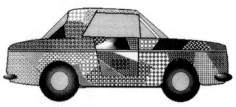

It can also be real cheap, especially if you can use samples and roll ends like I do. It'll only take you a few hours on a Saturday afternoon— or any day really, that's more or less up to you. But I think you'll be surprised and to a certain extent amazed at the way this looks when it's all done.

And the finish comes up real nice when you use a floor polisher on there. That's more of a pride thing because most linoleums have the no-wax finish so you can just damp mop any odd spill you get on it, especially if it's stuff from the kitchen, like teenagers throwing eggs at you out of pure jealousy. That's what that is.

But what you have is a one-of-a-kind, attractive automobile that looks good enough to dance on. I'm sure some of you Yuppies out there will be wanting to try parquet or ceramic tiles, but the technique is basically the same.

Remember, if the women don't find you handsome they should at least find you handy.

Driving Song #21

`She's` `Full` `Of` `Rust`

`She's full of rust and the brakes`
`   are shot`
`The tires are bald and she shakes`
`   a lot`
`She burns a lot of oil and she's`
`   hard on gas`
`But I got thirty-seven more`
`     payments, so I'll be keeping her.`

HER CAR, YOUR FAULT

She scrimped and saved her own money for two years to buy that car. She did not give you permission to drive it. But you just had to go behind her back and take it for a drive anyway, didn't you? And you just had to go to a lumberyard and pick up two sheets of drywall and then try to jam them into that tiny little hatchback. And you just had to rip the upholstery on the roof. Now what are you going to tell her? Well, you're not going to tell her anything...not yet.

First thing you gotta do is ditch the drywall, hop back in the car and go pick up her three nephews. Yes, those three rotten, destructive children of Satan. Take them out somewhere for ice cream and pop and chocolate. Lots of chocolate. And make sure they spend at least an hour in her car. By the time those hyenas are done, your rip on the roofliner's going to look like an afterthought. That'll get you off the hook. How can she get mad at you? You were just trying to give her nephews a treat. It's not your fault they're destructive little sociopaths. They're family. Just like you.

POSSUM 911
THE AUTOMOTIVE HOTLINE:
MINIVAN

HAROLD: This is Possum 911, state your name and membership number please.…

DAVE: Name's Dave, #456792.

RED: Okay. What's up Dave?

DAVE: Red, I've got a real emergency happening here. We're looking to buy a new vehicle… and she wants to buy a minivan.

RED: Oh, that's tough…

DAVE: A minivan, Red. What am I going to do?

HAROLD: I don't see the problem here. Minivans are very sporty, they look pretty sharp. A minivan is a very practical, fuel-efficient mode of transportation. I'd like one.

DAVE: See? Red, I don't want to end up like Harold!

RED: Now Dave, I know driving a minivan is a little on the feminine side, but technology can save you. You can dress up that minivan with masculine accessories.

HAROLD: That's true. Just watch out for those custom wheel covers that look so gaudy, or the mud flaps with the outline of a naked woman on them, or the neon lights that go underneath and just waste energy, or the big air horns—like off a diesel train or something, or stupid mufflers that make a minivan sound like blub blub blub blub blub, or those tacky sun visors, or the ugly, huge sideboards and fender skirts, and the phony macho tailpipe extensions.

RED: Got all that Dave?

DAVE: What was the last one?

RED: Tail pipe extensions.

DAVE: Thanks… I hope we can afford all this.

HOW TO BE A GOOD PASSENGER

(Because Your Life Matters)

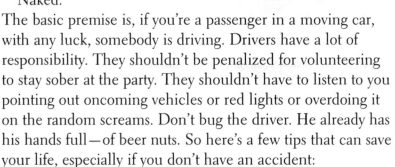

One of the most important things to learn if you want to get along with Lodge members is How to Be a Good Passenger. Unless you enjoy being thrown out of a moving vehicle.

On a bridge.

Naked.

The basic premise is, if you're a passenger in a moving car, with any luck, somebody is driving. Drivers have a lot of responsibility. They shouldn't be penalized for volunteering to stay sober at the party. They shouldn't have to listen to you pointing out oncoming vehicles or red lights or overdoing it on the random screams. Don't bug the driver. He already has his hands full—of beer nuts. So here's a few tips that can save your life, especially if you don't have an accident:

SIT RELAXED

When you're hunched forward, with your fingernails dug deep into the armrest, frantically scanning the approaching horizon it implies that you are not totally convinced of your driver's competence. But you have to trust him. If he says he knows his way home in the dark and doesn't need headlights, then you have to trust his judgement.

WATCH YOUR TOPICS

It's often a good idea to talk to the driver. It often keeps him awake and stops him from singing. Just be careful what you talk about or it could be taken as an insult. In general, don't talk about traffic accidents. Don't mention your uncle who also drives with one finger and a beer gut draped over the wheel, and how he hit a pothole and jammed the turn signal arm deeply into his navel. Don't mention the fog or the ice. If the driver hasn't noticed them, you're better off to start a prayer and try to relax your shoulders while you brace for the impact. If you have to talk, talk to other passengers, perhaps about the weather, or if anyone has taken courses in first aid and trauma treatment.

DON'T TOUCH STUFF

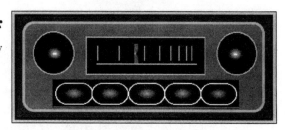

Just because technically you can reach buttons on the dashboard does not mean that they are legally in your domain of vehicular responsibility. The radio tuner and volume controls are Driver Only. As is the heater. The comfort of the driver is paramount. If he's warm enough, you just have to sit there quietly with your tongue frozen to the window winder. Don't touch the sun roof controls, the high beam switch, or the gear shift. If you have to adjust things or you go crazy, wear clothes with lots of buttons and zippers. Worry beads might help. You could also adjust the passenger seat a few times but remember, a little of that goes a long way.

DON'T KEEP LOOKING AT THE MAP

What kind of a message does that send? You think the goof is lost. And you could get motion sickness. Remember, vomiting never adds to the enjoyment of a trip.

DON'T GET EMBARRASSED

As a passenger you can sometimes get embarrassed by certain habits your driver practices—not signalling turns or splashing pedestrians or cutting across four lanes of traffic to run over an apple or sideswiping hitchhikers. Once embarrassed, a passenger is prone to say things to the driver that can lead to a difference of opinion and a 90-mile-an-hour hair-pulling incident. And any traffic expert will tell you that's asking for trouble.

Instead, wear a disguise like a false nose and glasses or, if

yours are already false, wear a real nose and glasses. That way other drivers will not be able to recognize you at the trial.

Avoid eye contact with other motorists, no matter how hard they're honking, or staring at you through the windshield, screaming, "Stop, please stop and let me off!" If you do accidentally lock eyes, shrug your shoulders to imply helplessness or hold up your arms so it looks like you've been handcuffed and they will assume you're being kidnapped and focus their anger and lawsuits on the driver.

Another good trick to deter angry people is to dress like a cop. Or even better become a cop.

RIDE DEFENSIVELY

As you sit quietly, watching the miles and bicyclists fly past your window, plan your escape route. Then you're ready in the event of an accident, or a really big guy getting out of an overturned tractor-trailer to come over and rearrange your driver's face. When you see an impending collision because

the driver is passing on a hill or bouncing off guard rails or jumping a lift bridge, pretend you dropped something on the floor, and when you go down to get it, stay there until the vehicle comes to a complete stop. It doesn't usually take long. Then, say, "Thanks, this is close enough, I'll walk from here." If the vehicle is on fire, it's okay to just say, "Thanks, see ya."

POINTING STUFF OUT

If you're older than 8, you should not be yelling, "Cow!" every time you pass a cow. The world is an interesting place, but you may distract your driver from oncoming traffic, oncoming guard rails, or oncoming canals if you keep up a running commentary like: "Oh look, that barn is burned. That must have been some fire. Hey, look at that apple stand you drove through. Hey, look at that cop waving at you… Look at that cop

shooting at you… Look a cow! That's some cow. She doesn't look happy does she? Maybe if you hit the windshield wipers, you'll dislodge her…"

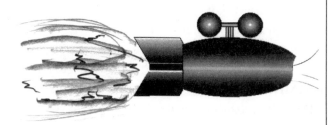

HOW TO HITCHHIKE

You never know what the highway of life will throw at you. Whether you've run out of gas or been run out of town, some time or other you're going to have to hitchhike.

Here are a few pointers:

- **TRY TO LOOK GOOD.** Comb your hair, hide the rips in your clothing with your hands and tuck your beard inside your lips. If you haven't bathed in recent memory, rub yourself down with mint leaves found growing along the side of the road. Don't confuse the mint plant with poison ivy. Nobody will stop for a hitchhiker who is wildly scratching himself. That's the voice of experience.

- **LOOK FRIENDLY.** Give oncoming cars a big smile. Show your teeth if they're handy. If you feel like waving, remember to unclench your fist. And use at least two fingers. If you're a guy, don't try to attract cars by showing cleavage. Any cars that stop are not ones you should be getting into. When a car passes you by, don't start swearing at him and flipping him the bird, unless you're sure the next driver can't see you. The image you want to project is that you're a friendly, interesting, unarmed passenger looking for a driver who likes people, light contemporary rock and long drives in the country.

- **BE AWARE THAT DRIVERS ARE TURNED OFF BY LITTLE THINGS.** Such as: If your hair is one amorphous blob rather than individual strands. If you're carrying automatic weapons. If you have steam or liquid coming out of your backpack. If your ankles are shackled. If your chainsaw is running. If your pants are in a nearby tree. If a nearby tree is now in your pants. Again, trust me on this, you'll wait for days for a ride.

- **YOU NEED THE SYMPATHY RATHER THAN THE CONTEMPT OF DRIVERS,** so try to look like you're temporarily out of luck, rather than permanently out of alternatives. Carrying an empty gas can is good because it implies you have a car somewhere. A shirt and tie suggests that hitchhiking was an unplanned exercise. When cars approach shrug your shoulders like, "Can you believe this?" They just might.

- **IT'S GOOD TO CARRY A SIGN THAT CLEARLY DEFINES YOUR DESTINATION.** And it should be somewhere on earth. Your sign should be neat. Not written in blood or lipstick. It shouldn't say, "I'm going out West where I belong" unless you're Wilbur Harrison. If you're going to Las Vegas, have the sign say "Las Vegas" rather than "Somewhere where prostitution is legal" or drivers won't pick you up because they'll assume you're a politician.

- **HOLD YOUR ARM STRAIGHT OUT LIKE YOU'RE PROUD OF IT.** And have your thumb pointing up. That's important. A thumb pointing down can be taken as a comment on the person's car. If the shoulder is narrow, don't be too proud to pull your arm in as the car goes by. Very few thumbs can stand even a low speed automotive collision.

Generally, if hitchhikers expect people to give them a ride, then they really should stop beating, robbing and killing those people. I'm sure it's a case where the few are spoiling it for the many, but until hitchhikers have a formal organization with a clear code of behavioural ethics and a meaningful lobbyist in the seat of government, it will continue to be one of the least reliable forms of transportation, just ahead of the Ford Pinto.

SHORT CUT

In an emergency, panty-hose can be used as a fan belt. Remember to take them off first.

YOU ARE WHAT YOU DRIVE

From Batman to James Bond, when you own a vehicle, it tells the world something about you. Here's a handy chart to let you know what personal message your vehicle is sending to the world and how to read messages that other people's vehicles are sending you.

VEHICLE	MESSAGE
LATE MODEL SPORTS CAR	Single. Impulsive. Salesman. Will have three different jobs during the term of the car lease.
LATE MODEL TWO-DOOR SEDAN	Recently married. Don't want to have kids.
LATE MODEL FOUR-DOOR SEDAN	Married with two kids. Still don't want to have kids.
LATE MODEL STATION WAGON	Married with too many kids. Always listen to your wife's opinion when buying a car.
LATE MODEL MINI-VAN	Married with too many kids who still need to be driven everywhere, but are old enough that your wife can start her new business which involves delivering things that are too big for the wagon.
K-CAR	Yet to hit mid-life crisis.
1986 HYUNDAI PONY	College student or Tupperware sales rep. Spends a lot of time alone. Waiting for the tow truck.
BRAND NEW HARLEY FAT BOY	Middle-aged. Balding. Beer gut. No chance with women. Now or ever. Take off the mufflers so you can't hear the laughter.
1957 CADILLAC COUPE DE VILLE	Elvis Impersonator.
AMBULANCE	Ambulance driver. Or hypochondriac.
TWO-YEAR-OLD ROLLS ROYCE	Former optimist. Conservative. Recently very money conscious. Your next car will be a Honda Civic.
CUSTOM BUILT IROC CORVETTE	One eyebrow. Hairy back. Low sperm count.
TOW TRUCK	Tow Truck Driver. Or former Lada owner who decided to cut out the middleman.
OLD CAR THAT BARELY RUNS	Lodge member.
USED VOLVO	Dink.
1968 RAMBLER	Your father is also a dink.
POSSUM VAN	A man's man. Major stud. Local hero.

```
Possum Lodge Traffic Bylaws:

#5. Obey all traffic signs.
    For those of you who
    claimed you couldn't read
    the traffic signs because
    you were dyslexic, I've
    added signs that read
    POTS, DLEIY, and GNIKRAP
    ON. So PJ NETRAMS!

Obey these Bylaws or face my
    frown. I'M SERIOUS!

    --Officer Noel Christmas
```

DRIVING WITH ATTITUDE

In the same way that your clothes and your grooming and your gun collection define who you are, so does your driving. The meek shall inherit the slow lane. Drive with Attitude.

PEELING RUBBER

Nothing says "man on the go" like sixty feet of blue smoke and a neighbourhood-piercing squeal. Sure it cuts down on tread life, but hey there's a lot of rubber on those tires and you don't know how long you'll be driving, what with the price of gas and the licence suspensions.

If your car doesn't have the power to spin the tires, crimp the rear brake lines and rev her up with your foot on the brake pedal. The front wheels will hold her back and the back tires will be wailing like a banshee. (Not recommended for front wheel drive vehicles.)

Laying a black streak across the road is more than just decorative; use rubber-peeling to intimidate other motorists. When you're at a red light, step on the brake (see above) and rev the engine until the tachometer needle moves as far as it can in a clockwise direction, preferably disappearing below the bottom edge of the control panel. Jerk your foot off the clutch so that it pops up. Hang on to the steering wheel and hold your breath until the smell dies down, just as you do in your normal daily activities. Release the brake and try to stay on the road. Don't worry about other drivers—they usually get out of the way. Just another upside when you're driving with attitude.

SPEEDING

Speeding is a natural phenomenon. People who aren't sure where they're going must speed to arrive on time. Driving is an entrepreneurial process, full of negotiation and strategic positioning, with no limits. Especially speed limits.

Speed limits are the result of a lack of speeders. If everybody speeds, the government will raise the limit. After all, remember how the government got rid of prohibition and the death penalty. And remember how much that helped your family. So remember, every time you get a speeding ticket, it's your fellow drivers who are letting you down. They need to tap into that "pedal to the metal" attitude. You'll never hit a car you've passed. Put the hammer down. And if you get caught, I never heard of you.

TAILGATING

A natural progression from speeding is the practice of tailgating. There is no better way to inform another driver that he's not going fast enough and has become a hazard to traffic than for you to rest your hood ornament up against his trunk lid.

To tailgate properly you should be able to read all of the dials on the other guy's dashboard. The sweat on the back of his neck is another sign you're close enough. After various turn signals and hand signals, he should pull over and let you pass but even if he doesn't, his slipstream is helping your gas mileage, and you can turn off your own headlights and just use his. The only way you can have an accident is if you're not following close enough. As long as you're resting against him, you can't possibly collide with him.

MERGING

Occasionally a highway is under construction or there's been an accident or the police are pulling cars over just because they can, and this often means that two lanes of traffic have to merge into one. Some drivers believe this should be done in a fair, orderly way, but who has that kind of time? Instead, cruise onto the shoulder and then rocket past all the cars and then cut in front of somebody and then wave thanks. Occasionally you'll find yourself embroiled in a game of chicken where the guy you're trying to cut off recklessly speeds up so you can't get in. In this situation, always try to cut off a car that's more valuable than yours. If you're a Lodge member, you should have plenty of choices.

FOCUSSING ON DRIVING

The most effective way to drive with attitude is to focus all of your concentration on the three basic fundamentals—the gas, the brakes and the steering. Don't let yourself get distracted by the peripheral controls like the horn, windshield wipers, lights and turn signals. Keep them guessing. In the Age of Information, the more data you keep to yourself, the more power you have. So drive fast, drive hard, and always carry your insurance agent's home number.

Possum Lodge Traffic Bylaws:

#4. Obey all posted speed
limits. And not just as
you drive past the posted
speed limit sign. Also,
knocking over the posts
with your bumper does NOT
mean the limits are no
longer posted.

Obey these Bylaws—
or face my frown. I'M SERIOUS!

—Officer Noel Christmas

Mr. Fixit

I want to talk to all you ladies to help you understand the things us men do. For example, the way we fix things with duct tape. Like say the mirror that fell off the car. Now I know a lot of you would take the car into a garage and an hour and sixty bucks later, you'd have it fixed properly and looking good. Whereas your handyman does it in ten minutes with about 7 cents worth of duct tape, and it is some kind of ugly. But let's go behind the actions and try to examine the reasoning.

First of all, what is the value of the vehicle? Are we talking about an '81 Cordoba with four hundred thousand miles and a real bad cough? Does it make sense to spend 60 bucks on a car that you can replace for fifty? And why take an hour to fix it if it can be done in ten minutes? After putting four hundred thousand miles on this unit, you really don't owe it any more of your time.

And why repair the mirror back to original quality? It just makes the rest of the vehicle look bad. There's no sense in having the repair job last longer than the equipment. So instead of criticizing your man for slappin' the mirror back on with duct tape, why don't you compliment him on his brain power? After all, he now has fifty minutes to spare and an extra 60 bucks in his pocket, either of which he could share with you.

Take the cash.

ONTARIO
POSSUM
KEEP IT BEAUTIFUL

Don't Tailgate. This car sheds parts.

torquin' it up with

DOUGIE FRANKLIN

COMMONWEALTH gAMES

Hi ladies, Dougie Franklin here with my monster truck. This set of wheels cost me eighteen thousand dollars. The truck was extra. But she's a big one and that makes it all worthwhile. She's about 12 feet wide, but I'm not exactly sure of the height. Although last year I drove her through the underpass on the base line at about eighty miles an hour, so she's obviously not taller than the base line bridge. At least, not any more. I lost a whole rack of spotlights on that one.

But you gotta have a big truck if you're going to go into the competitions like we do. We've done real well at Carterville this season. We've won: Most Cars Jumped, Most Cars Crushed, Biggest Whiplash to the Driver, Largest Exhaust Flame, Loudest Backfire. And Most Extensive Automotive Fire at an Indoor Venue. So we're real happy with that.

Our goal is to represent Canada in the Commonwealth Truck and Tractor Games. That's always been sort of a dream, to compete at the Commonwealth Games against monster trucks from Australia, Pakistan, Nigeria and the Bahamas. And I think we will do real well there. They're hoping to get Nelson Mandela as the Grand Marshall.

SHORT CUT

Retro-fitting airbags to your car can cost you an arm and a leg, and if you crash and the airbag only saves your arm, you're down a leg on the deal. So here's how to get a leg up. Just fill the inside of your car with those styrofoam packing chips that look like albino peanuts. Have enough so they come right up to your chin. For short passengers, provide snorkels.

Hood ornaments serve no useful purpose on a car, sorta like seatbelts used to before that law came into effect, but nevertheless, the hood ornament can be the deciding factor when choosing a new car, or a used car, or a totalled-but-the-guy-only-wants-20-dollars-for-it-and-I-could-resell-it-to-the-junk-dealer-for-twice-that-much-Bernice car.

Hood ornaments used to be even more important than they are today.

When this flying fish hood ornament appeared on the 1947 Hupmobile, it was the talk of the town.

So on the 1948 model, the only change made to the entire car was a larger hood ornament.

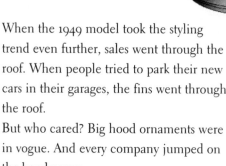

When the 1949 model took the styling trend even further, sales went through the roof. When people tried to park their new cars in their garages, the fins went through the roof.

But who cared? Big hood ornaments were in vogue. And every company jumped on the bandwagon.

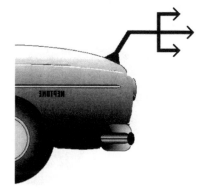

Back in 1951, when the Nash Neptune was unveiled with its trident-shaped hood ornament, I thought it was pretty sharp looking. Now, I have to admit it's just pretty sharp. There were a lot of injuries from this hood ornament, not when the trident first hit, but when well-meaning passersby tried to remove the pedestrian from the trident. Maybe if the barbs hadn't been so big...?

The fake cannon on the hood of the '52 Reo was popular until some people replaced them with real ones. Then the cops got all huffy.

In 1953 this UFO hood ornament certainly caught the paranoid spirit of the '50s, but it also caught the wind—lifting the front of the hood of the Studebaker.

With the Ford F-85 named after a fighter plane, one carmaker thought veterans of World War Two and Korea might enjoy this hood ornament, shaped like a tangle of barbed wire. It was not only dangerous to mechanics, it caught low-flying birds and was outlawed in 1955.

The 1959 Buick Le Sabre had a real sabre on the hood. It looked pretty dramatic, but again, it was rather dangerous to pedestrians. This was the first hood ornament that made the meddling, safety-conscious types think there might be a potential problem.

In the sixties it was common for American car companies to modify their cars for sale here in Canada. The way they did this was to give it a different name. A Canadian name. Like Laurentian or Acadian or Puck-mobile. And of course Canadianized hood ornaments were added, like this giant Canada Goose–a tailgater's dream in 1967.

Okay, this hood ornament is simply dangerous. Even I can see why it was banned. And the interim solution of just having it lightly bolted to the car so that in an accident it would fly safely out of harm's way wasn't much help.

Of course hood ornaments can be added to express the driver's political views, sexual orientation, or, in this case, religion. Here are the popular (but dangerous in an accident) duo of the "Christmas Tree" and the "Faith & Menorah."

THE CAR BUFFS ABOUT THE BEST CAR EVER BUILT

HAROLD

Our Car Buffs today are my Uncle Red and his best friend, Dougie Franklin. The letter reads "Dear Car Buffs, I am hoping you can answer a question which has been tearing apart my family and destroying my marriage. The question is this: What was the best car ever built?"

DOUGIE

Oh boy. That's a tough one. That really is one of the core questions of our time. It's an issue that strikes deep into the human psyche, I'll tell ya.

HAROLD

Which car is the best?

RED

A person's choice of car is like a window to the soul. Now, I have the Possum Van.

DOUGIE

And I have my monster truck.

RED

And Harold has his roller blades.

DOUGIE

You know, the Scandinavian philosopher Søren Kierkegaard claimed that free will means man can pass from the material to the ethical.

RED

And he drove a Volvo, didn't he?

DOUGIE

That's right, Red. But after opposing Hegel on the issue of determinism, he traded it in for a Saab. On the other hand, Heidegger, the German philosopher, argued self-awareness was intertwined with our sense of our own death, so he drove a Ferrari Testerosa. Bertrand Russell, in his work "**An Inquiry into Meaning and Truth**" argues quite forcefully for the Cadillac Coupe de Ville, while Descartes, had he lived in this century, I think would have driven a simple Ford Station Wagon.

RED

So ultimately Dougie, even the greatest philosophers can't agree on which car is the best.

DOUGIE

Which of course really ticked off the logical positivists.

RED

I'll bet.

DOUGIE

In fact, I think Jean Paul Sartre was closest in the existentialist view. Sartre drove one of those little Renaults that come in a kit that you build yourself, you know, in an attempt to know the unknowable. But the instructions that came with the car involved a tautological logic loop, and he never finished the rear suspension. But eventually Sartre figured out that essence precedes existence, so "best" is a subjective measurement, based on the observer's frame of reference.

RED

Right.

HAROLD

...So?

DOUGIE

So the best car for Red is the Possum Van, for me it's my monster truck, and for you it's roller blades.

HAROLD

Oh. Kinda makes you wonder what kind of car Plato would have driven.

DOUGIE

...A Buick Le Sabre.

HANDYMAN CORNER

BUILD YOUR OWN DRIVE-IN CAR

Have you ever had a friend or relative come back from a vacation and then force you to watch their slides? After the first hour you start empathizing with serial killers. But the sad thing is that even when you have real good holiday pictures, like my slides, you still can't get anybody to come over to your house and watch 'em.

What the world needs is a portable projection system—I'm not talking about a slide projector on wheels. No sir. I'm talking about your very own self-contained drive-away, drive-in theatre, made out of your car.

Your guests will sit in the car, just like at a drive-in. But the screen will be mounted on the inside of the hood, and when the hood flips up, forward, the screen's in position.

(If you have a car where the hood opens the other way, just whale away at it with a ten-pound sledge hammer and then re-attach it properly with the Handyman's Secret Weapon—duct tape.)

Hang your screen on the inside of the hood. You can use a bedsheet or, if you prefer something white, I suggest a fridge door.

Mount your slide projector on the rear deck behind the back seat. (You may have to move the dog with the blinking eyes.) Attach the power cord to the car's battery.

While you're in there, dump a bag of unpopped popcorn kernels into

the hole in the exhaust manifold. Once you start the engine and the manifold heats up, the popcorn will pop and be blown out the exhaust. You can catch it by clipping a pair of pantyhose over the end of your tailpipe.

Keep cold drinks and chocolate bars in the trunk and you have your very own portable drive-in slide theatre. (If you are ever pulled over by the police, be sure to tell them that this was all your idea.) **Remember, if the women don't find you handsome, they should at least find you handy.**

BAD SOUNDS

Nobody likes to be driving down the highway and suddenly hear bad noises and scary sounds. Especially if they're coming from the car. It's always a good idea to tell the mechanic what you think the problem is because he doesn't care.

So here are some sounds your car may make, and what they mean.

SOUND	POSSIBLE CAUSES
Chug chug chug....	Dirty spark plugs. You own a steam engine.
Putta putta pop putta pop	The engine's timing is off.
"Not on our first date."	Your timing is off.
GRIND GRIND GRIND	Your transmission is shot. Your car's transmission is shot. Your 8 Track player is shot. You've been shot.
Wuh wuh wuh wuh…	Flat tire on the car. Rap song on the radio.
Screeeeeeeeechhh....	Fan belt needs to be tighter. Alternator belt needs to be tighter. Grandpa's seatbelt needs to be looser.
(TOTAL SILENCE)	Dead battery in your car. Dead battery in your hearing aid.
Ping, Ding, Zap, Ping	Short circuit in the electrical system. Kid playing Gameboy in the back seat. Euro-pop song on the radio. (dance mix)
Wobble wubba wobba	Front end is over-steering. You are overeating. Car is made of Jello. Roadkill you ran over was stickier than it looked
Hisssssssssss!!	Leak in the radiator. Leak in the window. Leak in a passenger.

HANDYMAN CORNER

EXTRA HEADLIGHTS

I sometimes think about how to make driving at night a little safer. One way is to throw Old Man Sedgwick's truck keys into the lake. Another way is to take a minute and count the number of headlights on your car.

Usually, you come up with the number two which is not one of my favourites. I like the number eight. With eight headlights you can have two pointing up, two pointing down, two to the left and two to the right. The only way another vehicle can surprise you is from the back end, and you can eliminate most of that risk by maintaining a minimum speed of roughly a hundred miles an hour.

BAD

So, what you have to do is mount six more headlights on the front of your car, in such a way that they are solid yet infinitely adjustable and waterproof. Sounds like another job for the Handyman's Secret Weapon—duct tape.

Okay, after you've got all the headlights taped to the grill (and make them secure—use lots of tape and run it right back to the doors on each side), aim them as well as you can. They'll need re-alignment on hot days and after collisions.

GOOD

You're going to need extra power to run the extra lights, so line up a half dozen car batteries side by side in your back seat. Wire them in parallel using coat hangers.

(Metal coat hangers.) Attach them to the headlights with two or three sets of jumper cables attached end to end.

At this point some of you are probably thinking, "my wife will say it's ugly." Well if you've got an old garage door opener lying around (and who doesn't?) you can give this a real sporty look. Mount the garage door opener on the hood and attach it to a sheet of plywood (or half a ping pong table, for those of you who have keys to the Comunity Centre).

Hinge it with duct tape and now you have a European-style plywood spoiler, giving the effect of hideaway headlights as used on your Ferraris and Maseratis. If that isn't sharp, then neither am I.

Remember, if the women don't find you handsome, they should at least find you handy.

our trip to NIAGARA FALLS

It's just so common that when you have a great attraction in your own country, you never go see it. Like the U.S. with the Grand Canyon or England with Buckingham Palace or France with that nude beach. In Canada, we have Niagara Falls. It was Buster and Junior and I who went. Just for the day because even the biggest falls in the world are a tad repetitive after the first 9 hours. Besides, it's the Honeymoon Capital and I didn't want

Relax. That's just Buster's arm.

the three of us to have to share a room with a heart-shaped bed. Again.

It took us a fair while to get there because we had to travel through Ontario's wine district and everybody knows Buster there. We were sensible about the wine tasting stops. I was the designated driver and the other two were hammered out of their minds. We were pulled over by the cops and I was fine, but the Possum Van exhaust blew 1.5 on the breathalyzer. And here I thought the steering was loose. We got off with a warning because after smelling Buster's and Junior's breath, the cop was pretty much in the bag himself.

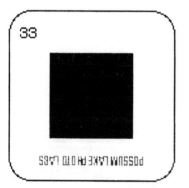

Have you ever seen that many corks in a person's ear?

They have a lot of beautiful flowers in Niagara Falls and most of them pop right back up when you run over them. I found a parking spot just a short cab ride away. I couldn't believe the noise and the spray. And after Buster and Junior were finished, we went to look at the Falls.

It's impressive. It's a lot of water falling down a steep hill. That's about it. Oh yeah, you get mist in the face. Which I like. Whenever I'm in a fight I prefer to get

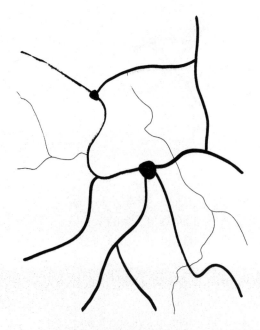

POSSUM LAKE PHOTO LABS

Here we are at the Falls, until the guard made us climb back over the wall.

missed in the face. Several Japanese tourists handed us their cameras and pointed at themselves and at us and golly if that isn't generous, giving cameras away.

We didn't stay long. There wasn't much else to do except see the boat that is the Maid of the Mist and the souvenirs which are the Made of Taiwan. The whole place has the kind of charm and warmth that just shouts, "Run by Organized Crime," and Buster and Junior were pretty hung over so

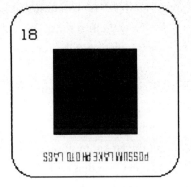

POSSUM LAKE PHOTO LABS

seeing that much water drop was

Buster's bow tie is made of cheese.

POSSUM LAKE PHOTO LABS

only giving them bad ideas. I rolled them into the back of the van and headed for Possum Lodge. We left the Honeymoon Capital and the honeymoon was over. As we bid adieu to the vineyards it was whine, whine, whine all the way home.

This is us going back for our shoes.

WHAT TO DO WITH THAT CAR HOOD

If you're like me, you often find yourself driving down the highway and then all of a sudden your car hood flies up and blows off. Don't you hate that? Probably my own fault for closing the hood with the same piece of duct tape over and over.

But lemme tell you, it's worth going back and getting that hood, even if you have to apologize to the people at the bus stop. That hood can save you thirty bucks come Christmas. With a little skill and ingenuity and some rope, you can turn that hood into a toboggan.

Now the first thing you need to do is put the rope through the front and tie it to something so it doesn't flop around when you're coming down the hill. Or get the fat kid to sit on it.

Now you don't want to just ride it by sitting down on the bare metal. You need

TIE ROPE TO HOOD ORNAMENT

USE PLENTY OF DUCT TAPE

CAR HOOD TOBOGGAN

to be a little higher so you can see what's up ahead because there's nothing worse than screaming down a farmer's hill and getting hit in the face with a frozen trail treat.

Okay, so pork the front seat out of a former friend's car (he shouldn't be driving in winter anyway) and strap it to the inverted car hood with the Handyman's Secret Weapon—duct tape. Now go out and have yourself some fun.

And make sure you really enjoy that first run because this unit comes in at around 400 pounds and you may not be able to convince the wife to drag it back up the hill.

Remember, if the women don't find you handsome, they should at least find you handy.

Bill's Tips On How To
THEFT-PROOF YOUR CAR

Howdy! For some people, there's nothing worse than having your car stolen. Personally, I think global famine, nuclear war, and any sit-com starring Alan Thicke are worse, but still, no one enjoys coming out of a store and looking around for their vehicle only to realize it's been stolen. Or repossessed.

So here are my proven tips to theft-proof your car:

- ☐ Install one of those anti theft "club" devices on your steering wheel. But be warned: never lock the club onto your steering wheel if you are still sitting in the driver's seat and you happen to be wearing very baggy pants with large belt loops and you drop the keys and you're on a very lonely road. Just trust me.
- ☐ Install a car alarm. Or if you're on a budget, just get the stickers.
- ☐ Always park beside a much better looking car. This is hard to do at Possum Lodge, but works well anywhere else.
- ☐ Remove your keys when you park the car.
- ☐ Remove the distributor cap.
- ☐ Remove the steering wheel.
- ☐ Put a dummy in the passenger seat. (Now you know why your wife lets you ride with her.)
- ☐ Paint your car to look like a police car.
- ☐ Paint your car to look like a Lada.
- ☐ Paint your car to look like a Lada police car. Crooks can't steal cars when they're laughing.
- ☐ Buy a car with a smashed up front end and always park it against a tree, telephone pole, or hydrant, so it looks like an accident scene.
- ☐ Install a transformer which converts your battery's 12 volts into say, 1 million volts. Then wire the transformer to the springs in your driver's seat. Hide a little on/off switch under the dashboard that only you know about, so that if anyone but you turns on the ignition, they receive an electrical surprise so strong they punch a sun roof in your car. But remember to hit the switch "off" when you get in the car, unless you're wearing rubber undershorts. Which isn't a bad idea. Trust me.

BiOGRAPhy
auto

- WINSTON ROTHSCHILD

RED

Welcome to Auto-Biography, where members of Possum Lodge share remembrances of cars past. Winston Rothschild of Rothschild's Sewage and Septic Sucking Services is here...

WINSTON

No tank too big,
No tank too small.
Teacup or swimming pool,
We suck them all.

HAROLD

Are we there yet?

RED

Winston is here to tell us about his first car.

WINSTON

She was a Ford. A Country Squire ranch wagon, with the real honest-to-goodness imitation wood sides. Those old Fords were great. The bodies would rust right off 'em, but the big V-8's would run forever. The new Fords, they don't rust like they used to. I miss that.

RED

Those station wagons were big, eh?

WINSTON

Yeah. I ran my very first business right out of that station wagon.

RED

First business? I didn't know that, Winston. I thought you were always in the septic business.

WINSTON

I was. Mounted a pump in the passenger seat, eh? Right beside me. And then with the middle seat folded down and the back seat down, and a pool liner spread inside her, that big old wagon would carry almost four hundred gallons.

RED

You'd carry sewage in the back of the car?

WINSTON

Only till I had enough saved to put a down payment on the truck. And I was motivated. That was the hottest summer on record.

RED

Boy, I'm betting that unit could get the eyes watering.

WINSTON

Yeah, it had a pretty good bite to it. I popped out the windshield and drove fast, so the wind kept it back, but I still break out in a sweat when I see a Stop sign.

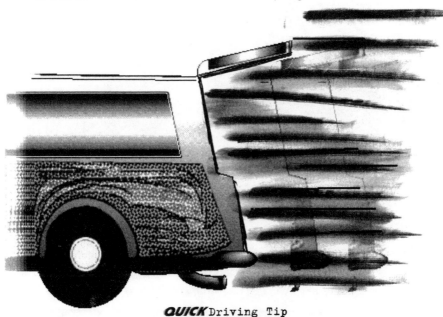

QUICK Driving Tip

In a Demolition Derby, never deliberately try to hit another car in the driver's door. In fact, that's good advice for your street driving as well.

TIRE TIPS

Tires are expensive. Why they can't make a tire that will carry a ton of metal at 100 miles an hour for at least 50,000 miles for under $10 is beyond me. That's just the kind of corporate gouging John and Jane Consumer have to live with. So here are a few tire suggestions that can save you big dollars.

no name tires

No Name tires can be bought at discount prices. Make sure you examine the tires carefully. They could be seconds, and in a race against time, you want more than seconds. On the other hand, they could be perfectly good tires that just didn't sell for some reason. Maybe the white walls are more of an off-white than white, or maybe the word ply is misspelled or maybe the treadmark says "I'm a Dork." Chances are these tires were made in the same way and in the same factory as the expensive tires. They are every bit as good. Look for Made in USA or Made in Japan. Avoid Made in Madagascar.

And be careful that they are not in fact homemade tires from somebody's basement rubber manufacturing kit. Is the brand just a guy's name like Bob or Herbie? Are there tools sticking out of the sidewalls? Are the treads in the same pattern as a pie crust? Is the tire made from a bunch of erasers glued together? When you come over the crest of a hill at 80 miles an hour to find a flock of sheep on the road, you'll be sorry you went with the Herbie Stove Bolted Roadial.

USED TIRES

Used tires are your cheapest source of quality rubber. If you're not concerned about all four tires being exactly the same colour or shape or size or for the same vehicle, you can pick up hundreds of free tires just by going to a mall after dark with a pile of trunk keys. Most people never use their spare and being at the mall proves they're shoppers, so they'll probably thank you for the extra trunk space. Just stay clear of those little Space Saver spares. They can make your Lincoln Town Car look like a hippo in high heels.

MAKING YOUR TIRES LAST LONGER

- When a car is standing still, 90% of the tire is not even touching the ground. There is no more effective way of making your tires last than by not moving your car. If for any reason you do have to move the car, don't forget the Laws of Physics. Particularly the tangential and centrifugal forces exerted on a rotating object. What this means is the faster your tire is spinning, the rounder it becomes. And the rounder it becomes, the less contact it has with the road. The less contact with the road, the longer the tire will last. The ultimate would be for the tire to have no contact with the road. (Yes, it's true that many accidents have occurred when a vehicle loses contact with the road, but on the upside, the tires are often in very good condition for resale)

   At rest, the tire is almost flat on one side. At 800 miles an hour, it is believed to be perfectly round. (Although nobody's ever had the guts to lean out and look.) So if your car can't be at rest, you should try to get as close to 800 miles an hour as possible. (Drivers who commute down Mt. Fuji rarely complain of tire wear.)

- Don't use a garage in winter. A frozen tire lasts longer. Plus there's a better chance your car won't start and that's the ultimate tread saver. (see above)

- Alter your driving patterns to suit your tires. Brand new tires in peak condition are designed to handle the roughest road conditions, from huge pot holes to fresh, sharp gravel. As the tire tread wears, all you need to do is change where you're driving. Switch to only the absolute smoothest of roads to make it easier on the tire. When even that's getting dicey, move to the sidewalks which are smooth cement, and when your tires are on their last legs, drive into town across your neighbours' lawns.

- Make your tire puncture-proof by letting out the air and removing the bleeder valve on the tire and then take your caulking gun and inject about 43 tubes of bathtub sealer into the tire. Now when the tread wears out, you'll still have lots of rubber to go on.

And even when your tires are finished, you can still use them to make lawn ornaments or driveway liners or soup bowls or earrings. Cover your home with tire art as a statement to the world—"I may be bald with bulges in the side and a lot of miles on me, but I can still give you a belt, so tread lightly."

Or it might just say "I need stronger medication."

ANOTHER WORD
FOR THE YOUNG DRIVERS

I know a lot of you teenagers would kill to have your own car, but I'm hoping that won't be necessary. Cheap cars are always available through one of those Drug Lord used car dealers or through the police or just call up the hospital and see if anybody who's in intensive care would like to sell their car. Just as long as you're not picky about the make or the colour or the stains on the seats.

Once you get the car, fill out the insurance form and list your grandmother as principal driver. Get yourself a part-time job at the gas station and take a couple of gallons of your work home with you every night. Make friends with one of the ratchetheads in auto shop and date a girl with money and you're gonna have the best summer of your life. You'll have some great stories to tell the judge in traffic court.

Possum Lodge Traffic Bylaws:

#9. If you accidentally back your vehicle into another member's vehicle, resulting in damages to said other member's vehicle, you are required to leave a note on the other member's vehicle. And the note has to say more than just, "Ha ha! I bashed your door in! Signed, Mr X." Include your name, licence plate number and insurance particulars, such as why you couldn't get a policy.

Obey these Bylaws—
or face my frown. I'M SERIOUS!
--Officer Noel Christmas

How to Use Your Car
TO GET WOMEN

by Buzz Sherwood

Nothing turns women on faster than a great car and nothing turns them off faster than the slob who's driving it. The trick is to totally accessorize your car so that it screams "Hunk," and then keep your mouth shut or the relationship will go "Thunk."

THE COLOUR

Women like flash. The kind of flash you do with a paint job rather than a raincoat. Paint your car a flashy colour, like, you know red, silver, deep blue. Avoid yellow, brown, and plaid. Be careful when choosing murals for your van. Horses and rock groups and space ships are okay, but paintings of nude babes tend to attract gay women or, worse still, straight men.

DECALS

Sayings on your car are a reflection of your personality. "I Brake for Stray Dogs" suggests sensitivity, but "I Brake for Stray Dogs when I'm Hungry" sends a whole other message, and "I Brake for Stray Dogs when I'm Lonely" is disturbing. You can send out the message that you're a worldly, well-travelled guy with bumper stickers that say, "Taladega Speedway is For Lovers", "We Saw The World's Largest Road Apple", or "I'd Rather Be In Go Kart Universe, Wisconsin." People generally believe that all signs lie, so having a decal that reads "I'm a Swell Guy" or "I'm Way Cool" or "Tested Negative" sends the exact opposite message. Something like "I'm willing to give Women one Final Chance. Apply Within" is the kind of challenge that women can't resist.

FUR

Fun fur seat covers. Day Glo pink or tiger stripes. Trust me, man. And don't just use old shag carpeting from your deck, or try stretching a velour sweater you got at a Star Trek convention. Spend the money and get the proper seat covers. They cost some bucks, but they'll save you a lot in flowers and candy.

WHEEL DISCS

Most women don't know the difference between, say, a 'Cuda and a Hemi 'Cuda. Like, it's true! But they do recognize a great set of wheel discs. If you're going out at nights, you can probably get away with a set of garbage can lids sprayed silver.

ADD ONS

Mud flaps on the rear tires and a big leather cover to protect the hood from stone chips sends out a message that you are a sensitive, caring guy. At least about your car. And a woman is gonna want to find out if you'll have the same respect and concern for her. (Even though every other guy she's met with a car like yours didn't.) The design on the mudflaps can make or break your chances. A top hat or dice looks very classy. A silhouette of a naked woman can be scary. Especially if you traced it.

LIGHTS

The more lights you have on that car, the better. Cover the grill, the side mirrors, the rear window, all the window trim, and get the fluorescent ground effects and even have a laser beam coming out your tailpipe. If the sun shines out of your exhaust, that gets respect. If you have enough cash to completely cover your car with lights, do it man. (Right after Christmas hardware stores sell off strings of Xmas lights for dirt cheap.) If you have enough bulbs, you can look like something out of "Close Encounters of the Third Kind," or that electric light parade at Disneyworld, or maybe even a galaxy. Stars give off light. If you give off light, you must be a star, right? (But maybe don't assume that hanging a moon will enhance this image.)

SOUND

LOUD! Jack up the car and look along the exhaust pipe until you see a section that's bigger than the rest. That's the muffler. Hack the muffler off with a pickaxe. Now you've got some serious engine noise happening. Next find a punk rock band that's bankrupt. That shouldn't be hard. If all you find is a punk rock band that's doing well, wait a week. Buy all of their equipment cheap or trade them for razor blades. Pile all of the speakers and amps into your back seat and hook them up to your

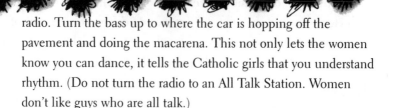

radio. Turn the bass up to where the car is hopping off the pavement and doing the macarena. This not only lets the women know you can dance, it tells the Catholic girls that you understand rhythm. (Do not turn the radio to an All Talk Station. Women don't like guys who are all talk.)

MAKE AND MODEL

Don't waste your money, man. Only other guys care that it's a mint 68 Boss Chevy Nova with Harley Carbs, and you don't want to attract guys, remember? Women couldn't care less what kind of car it is. No, really. Once women see the lights and hear the racket, they'll have made up their minds.

The deal is to find a way to not be ignored. If you deck your car out like I've described, the women will definitely notice. Even if they're pointing and laughing, you can sneak around on foot and join them with comments like "Look at that piece of crap. What a loser." Have a few laughs with them about it. They'll like you. You'll probably get to take them home. Call a cab. If you're lucky, you won't have to come and get your car till the morning.

```
Possum Lodge Traffic Bylaws:

7.   Members are responsible for
     picking up any parts that fall
     off their cars. If a car com-
     pletely disintegrates, as has
     happened far too often for my
     liking, the owner must remove
     it. Shovels are available from
     the tool room.

          Obey these Bylaws—
     or face my frown. I'M SERIOUS!

          Officer Noel Christmas
```

HANDYMAN CORNER

BUILD A JET-POWERED CAR

Here's a way to solve the next oil crisis. Switch to soap-box-derby style cars. To my way of thinking we need a smaller, lighter vehicle, made completely out of wood so it won't rust. Simple, but practical. Lightweight with excellent visibility, easy to park and there's only room for one person which will probably save a few marriages. You steer the vehicle with your feet which leaves your hands free to use as brakes.

The next question is what type of fuel-efficient engine would we use in something like this? I immediately thought of Roman candles, but they wouldn't sell me the quantities that I'd need to power this unit. Instead, go with CO_2 fire extinguishers. Point them out the back and attach them to the vehicle using the Handyman's Secret Weapon—duct tape. All's you do is squeeze on the trigger and the blast of CO_2 will propel you forward to the point where you should be able to maintain thirty miles an hour on a flat road, putting out fires as you go.

On a safety note I suggest you wear a scarf around your neck because you're sitting real close to the fire extinguishers and the CO_2 gets real cold. You wouldn't wanna be cruising down a major thoroughfare with a fozen head.

Happy gas-free motoring and **remember, if the women don't find you handsome, they should at least find you handy.**

WHAT TO DO WITH THAT CAR ENGINE

If you're like me, you hate to throw anything out—boxes, string, or automobile engines. I have an engine out back that I could take down to the scrap metal dealer and get a few dollars for it, but it wouldn't be worth my time plus the cost of gas, plus the work of putting the engine back into the truck first, so I could drive down there.

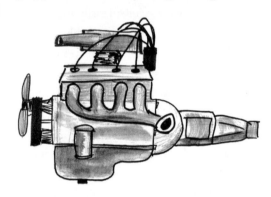

So what do we do with an old engine? Well, before you drive to a local park and dump it down a ravine, let me show you how one motor can outfit your whole kitchen.

Everybody who has space between their teeth likes corn on the cob. And parts from a car engine can give you an interesting way to serve it. Use a couple of valves as cob holders and fill up the valve cover with melted butter. Or 10W30 if it's to go.

The air filter makes a handy sauce pan for frying. And of course the lid comes with it. Fits perfectly and if you tighten the wing nut on there, it makes it into a pressure cooker. Just imagine that bursting at the seams with the smell of pressurized yams.

And I don't care how far you go, you're not going to find a better roasting pan with a built-in drain plug than the crankcase cover off the bottom of the engine. You roast a turkey in that and believe me, you'll taste the difference. It's greasy eating, but it's good eating.

If you're serving soup to a large number of guests, the exhaust manifold cuts ladling to a quarter of the regular time. Just line up the exhaust ports on the manifold with your four soup bowls and pour the soup up your own tailpipe.

And you were going to throw all this out. Where else are you going to find a free set of kitchenware that has over a hundred thousand miles on it? That's unique, isn't it? And Mother's Day is just around the corner.

Remember, if the women don't find you handsome, they should at least find you handy.

```
Possum Lodge Traffic Bylaws:

#2.  When a member no longer wishes to
     own a car, he is responsible for
     having it removed from Lodge
     property. This must be done by a
     certified tow truck, and not by
     hitching it to an unsuspecting
     member's rear end. Or the rear end
     of his car. Or by using dynamite,
     rolling it into a ravine or removing
     the wheels and calling it a shed.

          Obey these Bylaws—
     or face my frown. I'M SERIOUS!

          Officer Noel Christmas
```

GLEN BRACKSTON'S TIPS FOR HOSTING THE PERFECT TAILGATE PARTY

By GLEN BRACKSTON *of Brackston's Marina, Sales & Service*
with advice from MARTHA STEWART *of That Show I Can't Stand*

Okay, here's the thing. My wife got a subscription to *Martha Stewart Living* magazine. It's chock full of really useful ideas like "Make Your Own Personalized Dinnerware By Mining And Smelting Iron Ore You Dig Up From Your Yard." And my personal favourite, "Save Money By Making Your Own Vacuum Cleaner Bags From Papyrus Reeds."

Now normally I wouldn't have read a Martha Stewart magazine, but there was nothing else in the can that day, except the instructions on a tube of Preparation H, and I know those by heart. So I was skimming through this magazine, and I read Martha's "10 Tips For a Memorable Dinner Party." And the thing that killed me was that old Martha's 10 tips were the same ones that I use to plan a memorable tailgate party.

So here are Martha's tips, adapted for that special tailgate party.

1. **LOCATION IS EVERYTHING.** This is certainly true at a tailgate party. Try to park your vehicle close to the actual event you're supposed to be attending. Whether it's a football game or a stock car race, you want to be close to the action. Parking at a nearby mall, or at a roadside park five miles away doesn't cut it.

2. **GET THE INVITATIONS OUT EARLY.** Good advice. As soon as you've jammed your vehicle into a parking spot, set up as much stuff as you can to block other vehicles from crowding you, then start yelling, "Hey everyone, food!"

3. **DECIDE ON A THEME FOR YOUR EVENT. DECORATE ACCORDINGLY. COSTUMES CAN BE FUN.** Successful themes we've used at tailgate parties include "All You Can Eat," "Sauerkraut On Everything!" and "Bun Eating Race". If you pick the right theme, the decorating and costumes kinda take

care of themselves—for example, if your theme is "Beans" or if your team is playing in the game. Nothing looks more festive than guys with huge foam rubber hands and caps decorated with beer cans.

4. **CHECK WITH GUESTS IN CASE THERE ARE ANY DIET RESTRICTIONS OR FOOD ALLERGIES.** I always have a few light beers.

5. **GO OVER YOUR GUEST LIST. PLAN THE SEATING ARRANGEMENTS CAREFULLY. MAKE SURE SEATING IS WELL BALANCED.** Well, I don't really have a guest list because it's more a case of whoever drops by is welcome, but seating arrangements are very important. Arrange to have seating. Strong seating. Sure it's funny when some guy drops his 350-pound frame onto a lawn chair and it folds like the Buffalo Bills in a Superbowl game. But after you stop laughing, someone has to get the guy up off the ground. And don't let the guests just throw the doors of your car open and plop down on the seats. If two hefty guys sit on the same side of the car, there goes your hibachi.

6. **MAKE SURE YOUR COOKING AREA IS SET UP PROPERLY.** This also applies to tailgate parties. If you park your car on a hillside, you run the risk of scattering hot coals and food all over your guests. After a foot-long hot dog falls in the mud, it takes a long time to get it clean enough to eat.

7. **DECIDE ON A MAIN COURSE AND THEN PLAN THE REST OF THE MEAL AROUND IT.** Good point. For me, the main course is always beer. To complement the beer, I like to serve food.

8. **START WITH A LIGHT, BUT TASTY APPETIZER.** You gotta have an appetizer, or the guys will start eating the bratwursts raw. I've had success with bags of Cheesies, Potato Stix, Corn Bugles and Ketchup Chips. I've heard of people offering trays of veggies, but I can't see that working.

9. **SERVE A VARIETY OF WINES.** Ditto. Only it's beers.

10. **MAKE A SPECTACULAR DESSERT, AND GUESTS WILL REMEMBER IT.** Yeah. A huge bowl of Smarties is a big hit.

I have personally experienced a long line of British cars. The Morris Minor, the Austin 7, the Vauxhall, the Vanguard, the Envoy, and who can forget the Hillman Minx, no matter how hard they try? These cars have all been various levels of disaster. Although Rolls Royce and Bentley are arguably the best cars in the world,

the rest of the British automotive line-up is pretty pathetic. If you were grading British cars, there'd be a few A students with rich parents, and a lot of dropouts, drop offs and drop aparts. Britannia may rule the waves, but with cars, she waives the rules.

THE LONGEST JOURNEY BEGINS WITH THE CAR STARTING

Most British cars won't start in North America. It's too cold or too hot or too dry or too windy or too stressful or too provincial. They just don't build the cars for our climate. The battery is about the size of a pound of butter so you only get a few chances to get it going. Most people can't start their British cars and don't show up for work. In Britain, unions are very powerful. Is this a coincidence?

WHERE THERE'S SMOKE, THERE'S A BRITISH CAR

That cloud of blue smoke you see billowing out of that tiny British exhaust pipe is burned oil. In North America, the philosophy is to burn gas and lubricate with oil. In Britain, they burn oil and lubricate with beer. And you can tell by the smell of the blue smoke that oil is not a clean burning fuel. The problem stems from the looseness of the engine parts. The pistons flop around in the cylinders and the valves flop around in the guides and the oil flops all over everything. Maybe the price of gas is so high that they've switched to oil or maybe it's the only way to trace a getaway car when your police force is unarmed and on bicycles and all named Bobby.

But Honey, It's So Little

British cars are tiny. The bodies are tiny. But the windows are normal-sized. From a distance they look like a cartoon of a car, and Woody Woodpecker would not look out of place behind the steering wheel. The British cars are small because they're made for short narrow roads with quaint hamlets every three miles. Our highways are often 3,000 miles long and most of the drivers have never seen *Hamlet*. A little Morris Minor winding out at a top end of 63 miles an hour with a vapour trail of blue smoke is not going to fare well between a couple of tractor trailers with pup trailers jammed full of livestock. It's a tiny car with tiny lights whizzing along on tiny tires. Those tires would look oversized on a lawnmower. Imagine how fast those tires are spinning on the highway. You could have four flat tires and not even know it till you slowed down. British cars are made with thin sheet metal and virtually no safety features except big windows that you can easily fly out of and hopefully land in a quaint British haystack. So if you're driving one of those cars, you are out on the highway in a ball of foil. If you have an accident, your car will be scrunched up and thrown in the ditch like a chip bag. A British chip bag—oil and vinegar.

Different Countries, Different Cars

The fundamental problem with British cars in North America is the difference between the geography and culture of the nations. Britain is about the size of a mall. There's nowhere to go and all the time in the world to get there. Another point is that the British are extremely class conscious. It's only right and proper and traditional that the lower classes should have crappy cars, while the aristocracy gets the peaches de la cream. In North America we are far more equal and democratic—here everyone gets crap.

The Bottom Line

The British are fine people and really funny to listen to, but their cars don't have a chance. This is not their finest hour. It's time for them to keep a stiff upper lip and announce to the world that they are finally giving up on the automotive industry and are going to buy Japanese cars like the rest of us.

This car stalls at the speed limit.

Great Car Names For Great Cars

by Winston Rothschild II
OF ROTHSCHILD'S SEWAGE AND SEPTIC SUCKING SERVICES
"The One To Know When You've Got Overflow"

Car names are thought up after the car is designed. The designers design the car and then the advertising guys look at the design and they think of a name that really captures the car's image. Like "Viper." Or "Firebird." Or "Edsel."

And then they test out the name. They do surveys and opinion polls and marketing tests. Like they'll ask people, "Would you buy a car named Crapmobile?"

But even then, they make mistakes. The Chevy Nova didn't sell in South America cause in Spanish, No-Va means No-Go. Who's gonna buy a No-Go? Apparently not even Bolivians.

So what is my point? Well, I guess what I'm saying here is that you can't be too careful when you're choosing a name.

I even drew up this list to show you how similar names are good or not good.

GOOD	NOT GOOD
Mercury Sable	Mercury Animal Pelt
Volkswagen Scirocco	Volkswagen Hot Air
Acura Legend	Acura Bullroar
Ford Pinto	Ford Clydesdale
Viper	Rattler
Malibu	Cleveland
Lumina	Enema
Chevy Citation	Chevy Parking Ticket
Lincoln	Eisenhower
Ford Tempo	Ford Beat
Pontiac Sundance	Pontiac Slamdance
Ford Probe	Ford Rectal Thermometer

You can start to see why some cars never had a chance. The Tucker? Sounds like a serviette. The Hupmobile? Sounds like it has hiccups. And Studebaker is just way to close to Stupid-bugger.

Thank you.

Signed, Winston "Hose Boy" Rothschild.

IMPROVING YOUR GAS MILEAGE

Ever since the oil crisis in the mid-seventies, people have been concerned about gas mileage. Here are a few tips that you won't get from the EPA, the NRA, CSIS or the CIA.

SAVE MONEY ON GAS

$ An average tank of gas costs about $30. An average gas syphon costs $7.95. Do the math.

$ Hang out at self-serve gas stations with a gas can. While a guy is going up to pay, squeeze yourself a can-full out of his pump.

CONSERVE GAS

$ Magnetize your front bumper. Pull onto the highway and tailgate. Shut your engine off. Don't start your car until you come to your exit. You'll save a fortune.

$ Don't go anywhere that isn't downhill. This means you have to come home by a different route. And it won't be your home. But that may not be a bad thing.

$ Turn the engine off every time you're coasting or stopped. (Make sure you have a good battery.)

$ Pretend you don't have a good battery and ask people to push-start you. Just keep yelling, "Almost! Almost! A bit faster!" And let them just push you to the mall. If they complain, point out how good an aerobic workout they've just had without having to pay expensive membership fees to a health club.

$ Car pool to work and be "sick" whenever it's your turn.

$ Take the energy-saver nozzle off your bathroom shower head and splice it into your gas line. This will restrict the amount of gas that flows to the engine.
(Don't try to pass on a hill.)

$ If you have an enormous, gas-guzzling, North American car, put it in neutral and tow it with one of those little Hyundai Ponies.

$ An engine uses very little gas when idling. Disconnect the gas pedal and idle everywhere. It's a great way to avoid high-speed accidents and to get attention from other drivers.

$ When driving into the wind, remove things that cause drag like hood ornaments and side view mirrors. When driving with the wind at your back, open your doors and trunk so they'll act like sails.

$ Experiment with alternative fuels such as methane, propane, rubbing alcohol, shoe polish and road tar.

$ If you have teenage drivers, you can limit the amount of gas they use by not putting any in.

$ You can reduce your own gas consumption by having your licence suspended.

ALTER YOUR VEHICLE

The more weight, the more gas. Just look at Moose Thompson. You need to reduce your car's curb weight:

$ Remove anything you don't really use. Start with the things you use the least: turn signals, curb feelers, spare tire, jack, passenger seat, mirrors, lights, gauges, hood, trunk lid, fuzzy dice, passengers, little ceramic doggie with the bobbing head.

$ Clean your car. I removed over 200 pounds of old candy wrappers, ripped maps, and coffee cups from under the driver's seat of the Possum Van. I would have got more out, but I use the bottom layers as my floor.

$ Inflate the tires with hydrogen. (Not recommended for fire trucks.)

$ Do not maintain the finish on your car. Rust is lighter than metal.

Aerodynamics is an important component of speed. That's why fat people can't run.

$ The most efficient body style is small in the front and big in the back, which pretty much describes most of the Lodge members and their wives. To get the front end low, try wedging your car under a tractor trailer at 40 miles an hour. To get the back end high, wedge the trunk lid open with a manure shovel. (Leave some manure on it to prevent tailgating.)

$ Make your car smooth. Lather it up with car wash soap and then shave it. Remove excess lather with a hot towel and then slap on a polymer-based skin bracer. Once a week should do it, but Italian cars may have to shave more often.

COMMON SENSE IS THE BEST SOLUTION

$ If you are honest with yourself and you have cable, you know that you really don't want to go anywhere to be with anybody and you really would prefer it if they'd do the same. Staying home alone is the most cost-effective way to avoid depleting the world's dwindling oil supplies. Be an anti-social recluse. You owe it to your children.

12 SIGNS YOU HAVE A BAD MECHANIC

Don't ask how I know.

1. He charges you a half-hour labour for opening the hood because he couldn't figure out the latch.

2. You tell him your car is a "Ford" and he's "never heard of it."

3. He opens up your transmission and whistles, "Wow, look at all the little bitty parts in here!"

4. His Certified Mechanics Diploma is written in magic marker.

5. He only has one tool. A borrowed sledge hammer.

6. He tries to inflate your flat tire with his mouth.

7. He tries to loosen the wheel nuts by hand and then announces, "These babies are really on here, I'll need a wrench."

8. You mention you had trouble with the dipstick, and he fires his helper.

9. He inspects your resonator and announces, "Look, your muffler had a baby!"

10. When he tries to replace your oil filter with an air filter, and it won't fit he concludes, "This must be metric."

11. A good mechanic will ask you lots of questions but, "Where's the engine?" should not be one of them.

12. When you drive up to the service bay, he's riding the hoist and yelling "Geronimo!"

DOING YOUR OWN CAR MAINTENANCE

You can save yourself a lot of time and money by working on your own car. Cars have gotten much simpler through the years. You don't have to set the timing or hand crank the engine anymore. It's amazing how a little common sense can save you so much money and give you the satisfaction of knowing that whatever goes wrong, you were involved.

CHECKING THE FLUIDS

Just like you do with your kids before every trip, you have to check the fluids in your car on a regular basis. The rad, the windshield washers, the power steering, the master cylinder, the engine, the transmission, and the differential are all things that are designed to have liquids in them. Similar to your Uncle.

And speaking of dipsticks, they are there to help you check the levels. Pull the oil dipstick out of your engine and wipe it off on your shirt. If it's a good shirt, wipe it in the armpit where the stain won't be unexpected. Re-insert the dipstick and remove it again. If you see any fluid at all on the dipstick, that's good enough. Yes, they have a mark for "FULL" which is supposedly the amount of oil you're supposed to have but don't forget that mark was put there by the oil companies. It's more of a marketing ploy than an automotive rule. Besides if

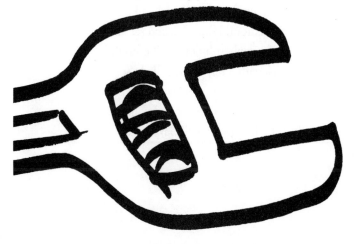

you're low on oil, the engine is obviously burning it or leaking it, so why throw good money after bad?

Some levels don't have a dipstick. The rad and steering box and windshield washer units should just be filled till they overflow. They each use different liquids but if you're stuck, light beer works well in any environment. Ask your kidneys.

The differential is the toughest. Remove the filler plug and if nothing drips out, you can assume that it's almost full and is probably fine. If you're driving along and it seizes up, locking your rear wheels and forcing the car into a series of donuts and figure eights on the highway, add more fluid.

CHECKING TIRE PRESSURE

If you don't have a proper tire gauge, use a pea shooter. Slip the pea shooter over the valve, drop in a pea, then tilt the valve to release the pressure. (Do not look down the end of the shooter to see if the pea is coming.) A tire at normal pressure in zero wind conditions can fire a pea 225 yards or lodge it 3 inches into a human buttock. (Don't ask.) If the pea doesn't go that far, or in fact drops into the tire, you need air. Inflate the tire until just before it explodes.

CHECKING LIGHTS

The hard part of checking your lights, after you get past the apathy, is checking the brake lights when you're alone. (If you're reading this book, you're probably alone a lot.) It's not physically possible to step on the brake pedal and be able to run fast enough to get around the back and see if the lights went on. There's a simple solution. Pull onto the highway and look for a truck with a big shiny grill. As soon as you pass the truck, cut in front of him and slam on your brakes. You should be able to see the reflection of your brake lights in his grill. (If he hits you, you'll have to re-check them.)

CAPPING THE COST OF CAR REPAIRS

There is a great wisdom in driving an old, worthless car, especially when it comes to car repairs. Always keep a close eye on the "Junk Cars for Sale" in your local newspaper. Another good source is news items like "Police Chase ends in Shootout." If you see a car that sounds like yours and it's for sale for $75, this amount becomes the maximum justifiable repair bill. For example, when your transmission gives out during a stump-pulling experiment at the cottage, you call and find out that a re-built transmission will cost $250, even if you install it yourself. Instead, just replace the whole car for $75 and keep the old one for parts. Repeat as often as necessary. You're saving a fortune and you'll end up with a huge parts supply. All you need is a big backyard to keep the cars in and, if you're married, real heavy curtains for the rear windows of the house.

ANOTHER BUMPER STICKER YOU'LL ONLY SEE AROUND POSSUM LAKE:

ONTARIO
POSSUM
KEEP 'EM

HONK IF YOU'RE A GOOSE
AND VICE VERSA

ANOTHER ¢heap Trick
BY DALTON HUMPHREY

Windshields cost money. Tinted windshields cost even more. a pair of tinted sunglasses is only 2 bucks at the drugstore. Think about it.

torquin' it up with DOUGIE FRANKLIN

Quads

Hi ladies, this is Dougie Franklin with a few words about my monster truck. Now she's got a stock windshield with a quad and a dual range ten-speed with a high torque sure grip rear end with a quad. Air suspension all around, load lifters, load levellers, load limiters, and a quad, fully loaded. The power plant is a double overhead cam fully blown, fuel injected, hemi bored out to 600 cubes with the big bite clutch, aluminum headers and two quads. And she is street legal. Except on small bridges and two lane highways. She moves though. She'll do a ton in first gear. A ton is a hundred miles an hour for anybody who doesn't know or hasn't ever done a ton. If there are such people. I can do a ton and a half on regular gas. Even more on ethylene. I was gonna set up the carb to run on testosterone, but the gas stations around here don't carry it.

```
Possum Lodge Traffic Bylaws:

#6. No wheelies on the
    driveway, parking lot,
    front lawn, dock, or
    meeting room.
        Obey these Bylaws—
or face my frown. I'M SERIOUS!

    Officer Noel Christmas
```

SEVEN KINDS OF SMOKE AND WHAT THEY MEAN

SMOKE FROM THE GRILL, RAD OR HOSES

This is actually not smoke. It's steam. It can be caused by one of two things —Something Being There or Something Not Being There.

The "Something Being There" category would include anything that would overheat the engine or impede the flow of water through the engine cooling system, such as a small dead bird or a work sock wedged inside one of the hoses; a 75-foot house trailer hooked to the rear bumper of a Nash Metropolitan on the up side of Pike's Peak; a gaping hole in the rad as a result of rear-ending a pole vaulter; a solid block of ice clogging the rad tubing (mainly in winter); the desert sun at noon in July; a large furry rodent-type creature imbedded in the radiator cooling fins; a thermostat rusted shut from never being serviced or replaced in the thirty years the car has been in your family.

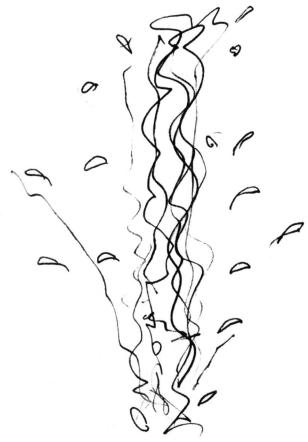

The "Something Not Being There" category would obviously include anything necessary to allow the flow of water, such as a complete lack of said water; the absence of anti-freeze in the water (see "solid block of ice" above); the missing drive belt for the water pump; the hoses you took off to make a tuba for your sister's wedding.

SMOKE FROM THE DASHBOARD

Unless you're driving an early experimental car that runs on wood, dashboard smoke is probably an electrical fire. In most cases it's caused by driver negligence: a spilled cup of coffee (or even more volatile liquid) or coins dropped down the defroster vents. Maybe you dropped tinsel down there on your way home from Liberace's estate sale.

Or maybe you've been impatient with the radio or heater performance and have randomly kicked up under the dashboard with steel-toed shoes. Perhaps you've driven through piles of leaves for fun, and you have shredded, dried pinecones on the red hot heater core.

In any case, you have a short circuit causing a wire to overheat and burn. It will probably blow a fuse and go out, or it could go out once the wire burns and opens the circuit, or it could turn into a massive automotive fire that totally engulfs your car. But you've got a 2 out of 3 chance that it's not serious, so just roll down the window and keep driving.

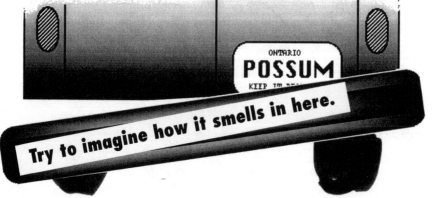

ONTARIO
POSSUM
KEEP 'EM ...

Try to imagine how it smells in here.

SMOKE FROM THE ENGINE CRANKCASE

When you see smoke coming out of the dipstick hole or the oil filter cap, that means you have a fire in the engine crankcase. If you're wondering what that is, think back to the oil fires in Kuwait. That's basically what's going on in there except that no one will help you put it out. The engine has overheated and ignited the oil, usually caused by an extreme shortage of oil, usually caused by you buying self-serve gas and not checking the oil for seven years. If you have a crankcase fire, pull over, remove the licence plates and all other identifying features, and find an alternative mode of transportation. (See tips on Hitchhiking.)

SMOKE FROM THE TRUNK

Unless you're hauling manure, this is probably a fire. Before you open the trunk lid, try to remember what's in there—a lawnmower? Fireworks? Any type of missile? Maybe you're better off to just keep driving and keep the fire behind you. It could be a while because the gas tank is back there, but on the bright side, nobody will tailgate you.

SMOKE FROM THE WHEELS

Smoke from the wheels is very rarely a fire. It is usually rubber burning from friction which, 90% of the time is caused by you pushing down too hard on one of the pedals—either the gas or the brake. Ease back on your stops and starts and that should remove the tire smoking problem.

It could also be that one of your rear wheels has locked up. That usually happens when an ordinary guy tries to change his own differential fluid. Remove the cover and look inside and you'll recover that wrench that you've been missing. Take it out and everything should be fine.

If it's the front tires that are smoking, you may have an alignment problem. Turn the steering wheel to go straight and get out and look at the tires. If they are pointing directly toward or away from each other, you need a front end alignment. And so does your car.

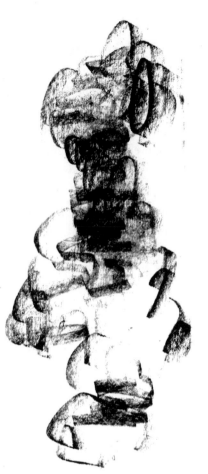

SMOKE FROM THE EXHAUST PIPE

If it's a cold or a damp day, this is probably steam and nothing to worry about. However if the smoke is black and full of charred metal slivers with occasional multi-coloured flame balls, there could be a problem.

The exhaust pipe is the off ramp for the unburned gases from the engine. Be careful what kind of gas you use. Don't buy it on the black market from a guy with a German accent. His prices are way out of line. And don't just assume that old cans of paint and hairspray and homemade beer will automatically work in your car. Take your exhaust problems very seriously. As all

mechanics and proctologists know, there is no better clue to how things are working inside than what comes out the back end.

SMOKE FROM THE BACK SEAT

When you notice smoke coming from the back seat, you have to remember if you have thrown anything over your shoulder in the last couple of hours —a lit cigarette? A cigarette lighter? A propane torch? Bowls of kerosene? The Olympic flame? A barbecue? Church candles? Roman candles? Cans of Napalm?

If the answer is no, then check to see if anybody's back there. If you find a passionate couple, find out their ages. If they're between 40 and 70, look out, it's smoke. If they're under 40, relax, it's steam. If they're over 70, ignore it, it's dust.

Driving Tip #107
DRIVING LIKE DAD

Okay, no one in your family has the nerve to tell you, so I will. I've seen you driving around town—turning without signalling or driving too slow, turning right from the left turn lane, parking your car half on the sidewalk. The fact is you're starting to drive like your dad.

There's nothing scarier than a little man in a big car peeking over the dashboard with a sour look on his face. Now some say losing your driving skills is just nature's way of thinning the herd, but I say "Give it up." And I say that, knowing you won't. Because every man I'm referring to figures I'm referring to someone else.

So here's the alternative: at your age you really only drive to your job, your lodge, your grocery store, the gas station and maybe your church. Plot each course out carefully and memorize all the proper procedures to get there using turn signals and brakes. Try and stay up near the speed limit. It's printed on big signs at the side of the road. Once you have that circuit down, you're not such a menace.

¢heap Tricks
BY DALTON HUMPHREY

A long time ago, when I inherited my dad's Le Sabre as part of a complex tax deduction that saved him quite a bit of money and put me in debt—not that I'm bitter... sorry, where was I? Oh, right. That Le Sabre had a few things wrong with it. Chrome was pretty well flaked off. Kinda like Dad. And the trunk didn't lock, because it had fallen completely off.

One door was rusted out so it looked like another window. Actually that was very educational 'cause you could see how the inside of a car door worked—how the windows rolled up and the door locked. Or at least how they would have rolled up and locked if they weren't rusted solid.

The car had other minor problems. Cracked windows all around. A rust hole that Dad called "my sun roof." None of the instruments on the dash worked. Neither did the lighter. Or the glove compartment. Or the radio. The speedometer was toast, and the odometer had o-died.

But still, that Le Sabre was in great shape for a car with just over a million miles on her. It just didn't look much like a Le Sabre. More of a Le Pocketknife.

But it ran.

Isn't that why you buy a car? To get from point A, (your home) to point B, (someone else's home) and then back to point A as soon as possible. Or better yet, don't go.

ANOTHER BUMPER STICKER YOU'LL ONLY SEE AROUND POSSUM LAKE:

IF YOU CAN READ THIS YOU'RE EITHER TOO DARN CLOSE OR MY BUMPER FELL OFF AGAIN

IN CASE OF AN ACCIDENT

(Cut this out and carry it in your car)

- Remove your seat belt. If you were not wearing your seat belt, remove shards of windshield.

- Check all your passengers and make sure everyone agrees on the same story to tell the cops.

- Check for injuries. If none, immediately decide who will fake what for the insurance.

- If there's any part of your car that is not damaged, but you would like to have repaired free, damage it.

- Extinguish all smoking materials including cigarettes, cigars, pipes and passengers.

- Retrieve all passengers who were not wearing seat belts from nearby trees, ravines, rockslides and from under vehicles.

- If there is gas or other flammable fluids spilled on the ground, mark out the perimeter of the spill with lit flares.

- If the other driver is behaving in an upset or aggressive manner, hit first and ask questions later. One bruise more or less won't matter.

- Make sure you have your licence, ownership and bribe money for witnesses.

ANOTHER BUMPER STICKER
YOU'LL ONLY SEE AROUND POSSUM LAKE:

IF YOU CAN READ THIS YOU DIDN'T GO TO SCHOOL AROUND HERE

Driving Tip #1010
ANOTHER VEHICLE?

So you got the truck you wanted. But that wasn't enough. You wanted a four-by-four as well. So you went out and bought one of those. But that wasn't enough. You also wanted something small and sporty. So you just went out and bought a sports car. Two-seater. No room for the kids or the dog. Now she got mad about that, and you should have let well enough alone. But no, now you've gone out and bought yourself a Hovercraft.

A Hovercraft? You tell her about this, your life will be null and void. Funny how a thing that floats can sink a marriage. Your only way out is to get her wishing that she actually owned a Hovercraft. So go hide it at somebody's house and then go home and wait for her to get in a good mood. Could be a while. OK, so do something that might cheer her up and get her in a good mood. Why don't you clean up the yard? Maybe tow away some of those cars and trucks of yours. Then start dropping big hints like "Hey honey? Wouldn't it be great to have a Hovercraft?" Or "How would you like a Hovercraft for your birthday?" Or better yet, buy up some swamp land and move the family there. Sooner or later she'll see the sense in getting a Hovercraft.

I'm guessing later. Much later. Probably not till the divorce goes through.

QUICK Driving Tip

Thanks to cruise control, you can fall asleep without slowing down.

ANOTHER BUMPER STICKER YOU'LL ONLY SEE AROUND POSSUM LAKE:

THIS IS MY OTHER CAR

torquin' it up with

DOUGIE FRANKLIN

Work & Play

Hi ladies, Dougie Franklin here. You know, I'm real proud of my truck, I'll tell you that. I use it to deliver meals to the various shut-ins around town. And you should see the looks on the people's faces when I deliver a meal by coming across the front lawn and handing it in through the second story window. Real handy for some of the elderly who have trouble with stairs. But I also supply meals to folks who can't afford them and it really gets me sometimes. There's something wrong with a society where some people have so much and others have so little. We've got our priorities screwed up if you ask me.

This truck cost me about eighty-five thousand. Fully loaded. I used to have a Honda Civic, but I went to one of those truck and tractor pulls, and we just didn't do well with it at all. But you kids at home who may have a large overpowered vehicle with outsized tires, don't try crushing cars. Leave it to the professionals. We get a lot of head injuries. A lot of head injuries. Did I say that? But anyway, it's good clean fun. And we're not hurting anyone. Unless they happen to be looking up the exhaust pipe when I start her up. I never knew toupees were so expensive.

QUICK Driving Tip

Don't carry extra gasoline in your trunk unless it's in some kind of container.

YOUR CAR IS LIKE YOUR BODY

It's been said that the secret to a long life is to find a good doctor and a good mechanic. Since I do my own car repairs, I also do my own doctoring, because a car is actually a lot like a human being's body. For example, Rear End Shimmy is pretty much the same in people and Plymouths.

Now before you raise objections, like "My body isn't full of rust holes!" or "There's still some springiness in MY seat!" let me explain…

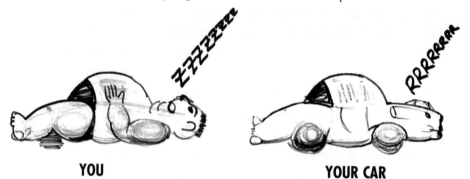

YOU   **YOUR CAR**

A car is a complex conglomeration of parts designed to get you from one place to another. Just like your body. A car is designed to withstand a certain amount of damage. Just like your body. Cars come in all shapes, colours, and sizes. Just like bodies. I'm kinda like the Possum Van. Harold is more of a K-Car. Moose Thompson is a bus. Old Man Sedgwick is an antique. And Stinky Peterson is an untuned diesel. I'm sure your family has its share of sports cars, station wagons and mopeds.

The car's frame acts like your body's skeleton, holding everything in place. Your skin is like the fenders and doors. And your guts are your engine compartment. Like your car, your body needs fuel. The only difference is with your car, it starts out as gas. And as you pile up the mileage on the highway of life, your car ages and becomes less reliable; it's harder to get it going and keep it running. Same is true with your body.

But one can stretch this analogy even farther, and since I have a lot of pages to fill up before they'll call this a book and cut me a cheque, I will. The fact is, every car part has an equivalent body part.

So if you understand how your car works, you can understand how the human body works. And vice versa.

BODY PART   CAR PART

BODY PART	CAR PART
Nose	Air Intake
Nose Hairs	Air Filter
Rib Cage	Engine Block
Lungs	Carburetor
Heart	Pistons & Cylinders
Blood Vessels	Hoses and Belts
Blood	Oil
Liver	Oil Filter
Stomach	Gas Tank
Gall Bladder	Oil Pan
Pituitary Gland	Gas Pedal
Testicles	Turbocharger
Spine	Transmission Hump
Belly Button	Hood Ornament
Leg Muscles	Transmission
Knees	Ball Joints
Feet	Tires
Toes	Tire Tread
Eyes	Windshield
Tear Ducts	Windshield Washer
Eyelids & Eye lashes	Windshield Wipers
Neck Muscles	Side & Rear View Mirrors
Brain	Electronic Ignition
Inner Ear	Steering Wheel
Facial Wrinkles	Odometer
Sweat Glands	Radiator
Sweat	Rad Fluid
Bladder	Rad Overflow
Fingerprints	Personalized Licence Plates
Intestines	Exhaust Pipe
Table Manners	Catalytic Convertor
Mouth	Horn
Ears	Radio
Tonsils	Fuzzy Dice Hanging From Mirror
Hands	Bumpers
Ring Finger	Brakes
Nipples	Bumperettes
Seat	Seat
Acne	Rust
Body Hair	Upholstery
Facial Hair	Chrome Trim
Anus	Car Salesman

HAROLD

Our Car Buffs today are my Uncle Red and his best friend, Dougie Franklin. The question here reads "Dear Car Buffs, I am thinking of taking the family on a vacation this winter. Are there any places you would recommend?"

RED

Golly there are so many. Moose Lake, Moose Factory, Moose Jaw, Moosonee...

HAROLD

I think our reader would prefer a place with less moose and more fun.

RED

Oh.

DOUGIE

Well of course you've got your Bahamas and the Barbados and your Bimini Island, and your Bikini Atoll, but I would highly recommend you check their weather and the food and the medical care at these tropical paradigms. Nobody can convince me that the best doctors in the world are working the resort circuit.

HAROLD

So where would you advise our reader to go, Mr. Franklin?

DOUGIE

Well before I signed on the dotted line for any of these tropical tours, I would take a hard look at a 65 or 66 Mustang.

RED

I don't believe that is technically a resort. Even with the heater on full.

DOUGIE

Well that's my point, Red. Instead of blowing your brains out on two weeks of sunstroke and diarrhea, why not invest those same dollars in a mint Boss 302 convertible? For the same price as a little fun in the sun, you can have it made in the shade.

HAROLD

That kind of misses the point of a vacation, doesn't it?

RED

Harold, if you had a mint Mustang rag top in, say, the racing green, you wouldn't need a vacation.

DOUGIE

Bingo. And any trip is just a flash in the pan. Once you get out of the hospital, you won't even let yourself think about it again. Whereas the automobile investment will give you daily pleasure and lasting value.

HAROLD

I really don't think you can equate the experience of visiting another country and/or culture with buying a used car.

DOUGIE

Harold, for what I spent on my monster truck, I could have travelled around the world four times. And what would I have to show for it?

HAROLD

Adventure. Knowledge. Memories.

DOUGIE

Harold, you can't crush cars with memories.

QUICK Driving Tip

In an emergency, you can drink the water from the radiator, but never <u>ever</u> eat that old chocolate bar under the seat.

our trip to JAMAICA

Didn't go.

our trip to SASKATCHEWAN

I think we went there. Not sure. Alberta was nice though.

our trip to DISNEYWORLD

We had a full load for our trip to Disneyworld. Buster, Junior and I were in the cab of the Possum Van. Stinky, Flinty, Scabby and Bubba were in lawn chairs duct taped to the floor of the cargo area, and Moose was up on the roof rack strapped down with bungees. We had no trouble getting across the border but the weigh station pulled us over and made us buy new tires. That really cut into our budget so rather than have expensive motel bills on the way down, we decided to get there in 24 hours non-stop. Instead of taking turns driving, we all drove all the time. One guy at the wheel and everybody else yelling suggestions at him. It probably wasn't the safest way to travel, but it stopped us from missing our wives.

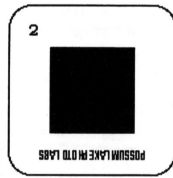

2

POSSUM LAKE PH OTO LA8S

Look at Moose on the roof rack. (That's not a tarp!)

We got to Disneyworld around 5 o'clock on the second day and went straight in. The parking lot sections are named after the Disney characters. The cars in front of us were parking on Dopey, but when the parking guy saw our van, he sent us over to Pluto cause that was closer to the Fire Station. We took the shuttle over to the main gate. We got in the last car and tried to make it "crack the whip." The Disneyworld parking people are friendly but they have no sense of humour and a surprising amount of upper body strength. We ended up walking the rest of the way to the main gate. We couldn't believe the prices. I was hoping we could get in as kids, but it's based on age rather than behaviour.

Here's Flinty watching a Topiary.

Once we got in and took off the extra clothing that we ripped climbing the fence, we went on everything: "Pirates of the Caribbean," "Twenty Thousand Leagues Under the Sea," "Tom Sawyer's Island." They even had a ride that reminded me of Harold's head—"Space Mountain." Moose Thompson was too big for most of the rides, but he went anyway. By the time he got off, everybody was singing "It's a small world after all."

The "20,000 Leagues Under The Sea" ride is actually a lot shorter than that, but lots of fun. The kid running it was okay, but he must work from a script, cause when we'd yell, "Dive! Dive!" or "Prepare to Ram!" Or "Fire Torpedoes!", he kinda froze up.

The Hall of the Presidents has a great show, put on by a whole bunch of Presidents. Half the guys thought they were real actors until we got up close and broke one.

Scabby got thrown out for doing this with Calvin Coolidge's head.

They say that movie stars are always so much smaller when you meet them in real life. But not Mickey and Minnie. Wherever you go they have all the characters from the Disney movies walking around, and they will pose with you for pictures, but as Buster pointed out, none of them actually talked, so I suspect these are not the same ones that you see in the movies. I defy anyone to see Moose Thompson and Goofy posing side by side and not think "Father and son."

The Bear Jamboree was a lot like a lodge party, only with less hair, and the Haunted House with the falling elevator scared all the other passengers, but we thought it was kinda tame after having driven down in the Possum Van.

We also saw the Swiss Family Robinson tree house, which is this ramshackle thing all held together with rope. Suddenly we were all homesick for Possum Lodge.

It was a great day—the rides, the food, the shows, the food, the roving entertainers, the food, and the parades, especially the ones with food. They actually have ice cream things in the shape of Mickey Mouse. But they taste like vanilla!

We had a small problem in one of the souvenir shops when Stinky Peterson had to explain how a mouse doll ended up inside his shirt. It wouldn't have gone there

5

POSSUM LAKE PHOTO LABS

Here's Moose eating another ice cream bar. Have you ever seen that many wrappers stuck to one face?

23

POSSUM LAKE PHOTO LABS

voluntarily. Stinky claimed he had paid for it, but when he couldn't produce a receipt, a large person of no specific gender or species, came over and took the Mickey out of him.

All in all it was a great trip and we'd gladly go again, but we're going to have to wait until we don't look anything like the pictures of us they now have on file.

This is us going back for our shoes.

ANOTHER ¢heap Trick
BY DALTON HUMPHREY

You don't need a car radio. In my Dad's day, when they wanted entertainment, they made their own fun. Which I guess is why they called it the Depression. You want music? Sing! You want news? Talk to your passengers. You want to hear one of those phone-in shows about all those people with their weird problems? Ask your wife about her sister.

THE POSSUM LODGE
Car Song Book

One way to pass the time on a long trip is to have a sing-along. But most songs only last three minutes and end up with everyone arguing over what the lyrics are. I've actually seen people come to blows over the words to "Blinded by the Light" by Manfred Mann. And you don't want to be in a van full of guys singing, "I am woman, hear me roar…"

The ideal song for a long trip is "99 Bottles of Beer On The Wall." It lasts for miles and miles. Everyone can remember the words. And everyone can tell exactly how long till the end of the song. On the other hand, "Row, Row, Row Your Boat" gets monotonous pretty quickly and leads to arguments over when someone was supposed to join in with their verse. That old classic "Hello Operator, Give me number 9…" might offend some passengers. And the popular "Hey there driver, speed up a little bit…" is lots of fun until you hit a guard rail.

Since we live in such a large country, with long, lonely stretches of highway with nothing to see except scenery and nature, it's obvious we need some more songs for long trips. So here are a few I've written. Enjoy.

FLUGEL HORN

(To the tune of "Who's Afraid of the Big Bad Wolf?")

Over there in Switzerland,
Switzerland, Switzerland.
There's a funny Swiss Brass band,
Swiss Brass band, Swiss Brass band.

They've played this way since they were born,
They were born, they were born,
By blowing on their Flugel Horn.
And it sounds like this...

(ONE PASSENGER DOES A TRUMPET SOLO WITH THEIR LIPS, MAKING
A LOT OF WET FUNNY SOUNDS WHILE EVERYONE SINGS THE CHORUS)

(CHORUS)

Flugel Horn, Flugel Horn
Bugle Horn, Bugle Horn.
Flugel Horn, Flugel Horn
Bugle Horn, Bugle Horn.

(REPEAT WITH PASSENGERS TAKING TURNS DOING THE TRUMPET SOLO.
THE GOAL IS TO MAKE THE FUNNIEST SOUNDS WITH THE LEAST SPIT)

NEVER HEARD OF IT

Driving along in our family car,
And we still have to go very far,
Looked out the window, guess what I saw
Sitting there at the side of the road?

Sitting there looking, oh, so fine,
On a post I saw a sign.
And so the sign I read
And here's exactly what it said.

(AT THIS POINT SOMEONE READS WHAT'S ON A PASSING SIGN)

Never heard of that before.
Sounds really dumb, oh what a bore.
Hope I never end up there.
Whatever that is, I don't care.

(REPEAT WITH A NEW SIGN)

EVERYONE BUT US

(to the tune of "LONDON BRIDGE IS FALLING DOWN")

See this car we're passing by, rolling by, rolling by,
See this car we're passing by, the people in it stink.

See the driver of that car, of that car, of that car,
What's he looking at us for, that stupid little fink.

Look at all those passengers, passengers, passengers,
All those pinheads in one car, kinda makes you think.

Let's all wave and they'll wave back, they'll wave back,
they'll wave back,
Look they waved right back at us, what a bunch of dinks.

(REPEAT)

THE GIFT

(Some songs are clap along or involve hand gestures and so
on. This song is sort of like that.)

I have a little gift I must pass on,
To the person on my right.
Will they pass it on to the next one along?
Yes, I think they might.

My little gift is free of charge,
I made it just for you.
It's very hard and very large.
You'll feel it through and through.

It's not like any other gifts,
If I may be so bold, Sir.
I make it when I take my fist
And punch you in the shoulder. (PUNCH!)

(CHORUS)

Pass it on. Pass it on. To the person next to you.
Pass it on. Pass it on. Your arm is turning blue.

(REPEAT FROM THE TOP)

THE DOOR SONG

(Here's another song that gets kids physically involved.)
    We're heading down the highway and we're way over the limit,
    If there's a car crash up ahead, then we will soon be in it.
    But meanwhile let's all take our minds off what fate has
        in store.
    By reaching down and pulling hard and opening our door.

    Click, pull, push it open. (EVERYONE OPENS CAR'S DOORS)
    See how the wind blows it shut.
    Click, pull, force the door open. (OPEN DOORS)
    We look like a car full of nuts.

    Flap our doors doing 95 (OPEN DOORS)
    And our car looks like it's flying.
    Other cars stare, but we don't care (OPEN DOORS)
    We're laughing so hard we're crying!

THE NONSENSE SONG

(This song was invented by Bill.)
(He says his family sings it wherever they go.)
(Sometimes they even sing it at the dinner table.)
    Wugga wugga wee woo where
    Digga digga didgery doo.
    Over there, Dad's nostril hair.
    I'm Captain Kangaroo.

    Lickety Lickety Lickety Split
    Drabble and drobble and drip.
    Axel Rose in the garbage pit.
    It's poison have a sip!

    Podunk Squeeze the Ketchup Bottle.

    Hubba hubba hubba hubba Arf!
    When it pops your thighs will waddle.
    Singing Polly woddle doodle diddle barf.

(CHORUS)
    Fare thee well, with your rubber bell
    Ding dong ding doing boing.

I just arrived and I'm not alive.
So I guess I should be going.

(Repeat until the lyrics start to make sense)

HOW MANY FACIAL TISSUES?

How many facial tissues are there left
   in this Kleenex box?
The label says there's five hundred,
But that sounds like a lot.

So far I've only pulled one out
But wait here is another.
I'll pull it out and lay it down
Here beside its brother.

(PULL OUT A KLEENEX, AND START AT TOP OF SONG AGAIN,
CHANGE ONE TO TWO AND SO ON. STOP WHEN YOU RUN OUT
OF KLEENEX)

ANOTHER Cheap Trick
BY DALTON HUMPHREY

*Three wheels are enough. Sure four are
better if you can afford them, but a
car really only needs three and some
weight in the opposite corner to stay
upright. Heck, it only needs two if you
have a good sense of balance.*

QUICK Driving Tip

Don't run over wild animals, especially if you
have to swing into the ditch to nail 'em.

our trip to
LAS VEGAS

The bunch of us had a weekend free and we were between seasons on the indoor and outdoor napping, so we decided to take a run down and try our luck in Las Vegas. Of course as soon as Old Man Sedgwick heard "run down" he figured he was invited. So we gassed up the Possum Van and headed off. I was driving, Buster Hadfield and Old Man Sedgwick were on the passenger side and Moose Thompson was in the middle and on both sides and some of him went back into the luggage area.

Here's Old Man Sedgwick. When we asked him to shave, we meant his face.

We didn't have much trouble crossing the border except for Old Man Sedgwick proving his citizenship. Apparently his birth certificate is kept in a humidity-controlled vault in the National Archives, but luckily he was carrying a tin-type of himself with John A. MacDonald back when John A. was just a kid.

We kept the radio going for most of the trip. We don't like the radio, but every time we turned it off, Old Man Sedgwick would start singing World War I songs and try spitting out the window without opening it. We got a speeding ticket outside Chicago. We were doing 30 in a 55 and the cars were backed up pretty good behind us. I had the pedal to the metal but with Moose up front flattening the tires, it was like driving straight up hill. We made it to Las Vegas around suppertime on the third day.

We pulled into the MGM Grand parking lot and pitched our tent right

Here we are giving the cuffs back to the cop. No sense of humour

beside the van. The parking attendant yelled something at us in Spanish. We thought that was pretty friendly for him to talk to us when he didn't really know us at all. We went to an all-you-can-eat restaurant. It went okay until Moose went up for the fourth time. They took down the all-you-can-eat sign and asked us to leave. I guess the manager was sad to see us go. He was crying.

We hit the casino but that was a disappointment. We wanted to play poker, but the minimum bet was $100 and we don't have that kind of money till we've played for at least an hour. So it was kind of a Catch 21. Instead we went to a revue featuring dancing girls. I'll tell ya, those women don't know the difference between a necklace and a dress. In hindsight it was a mistake to expose Buster to that type of sophisticated entertainment. Especially when he'd spent the last few days in the van with us. On the up side, the police were cordial enough as they escorted us out and they offered to drop all charges as long as Buster paid for every costume piece he bit.

We got up early the next morning and headed back to the Lodge. All in all it was a good trip, but the bunch of us agreed we wouldn't go again, even if the State Gaming Commission hadn't banned us.

3

POSSUM LAKE PHOTO LABS

Now those are what I call LEGS!

28

POSSUM LAKE PHOTO LABS

Buster in a dance costume.
(Those are REAL)

9

POSSUM LAKE PHOTO LABS

This is us pawning our shoes.

BiOGRAPHY
- Mike Hammar

RED

Welcome to Auto-Biography, where members of Possum Lodge share remembrances of cars past. Mike Hammar is here to tell us about his favourite car of all time.

MIKE

Oh, that's easy, Mr Green. The Corvette Stingray. What a set of wheels! Who could resist a Vette? Not me.

RED

Oh yeah. Beautiful car.

MIKE

Yes sir. I remember the first time I took a Vette for a spin. It was parked in front of a convenience store, keys in her, idling. Man.

RED

So you didn't actually own this car?

MIKE

Uh, no. But she was mine for an hour. And fast. She could outrun any police cruiser on the road. Man, that was a great car. I knew guys who would boost a Vette and sell it for parts. To me, that's criminal. Criminal. Cutting up a Vette.

HAROLD

Uh, perhaps Mr Hammar, you should remind our readers that any kind of car theft is not a good idea.

MIKE

Huhn? Oh, yeah. For sure. I mean I love Vettes, but I know now, a few hours of fun wasn't worth 2 to 5 in minimum security. No, I would say, if you want a Corvette, buy one.

RED

Yeah. But they're not cheap.

MIKE

No. But if you pick the right bank, on a Friday when they have a lot of cash

RED

Mike, remember how that ended?

MIKE

Oh right. No, you're right Mr. Green. I don't do that no more.

RED

Maybe what you should do is work hard, save your money, build up a credit rating, and then buy yourself a brand new Corvette. One you own.

MIKE

Oh sure. And then some loser comes along and swipes it for a joyride. No thanks.

QUICK Driving Tip

Always have at least one controllable body part in contact with the steering wheel.
(Preferably your own body part.
And your own steering wheel)

WANT AD

For sale: A collection of 250 automobile radio antennas. I'm selling this incredible collection under the conditions of my parole for vandalism. All money raised goes to the insurance companies. I'd rather not break up this unique collection, but if you recognize your antenna, I have to let you have it.

My attitude beats your right-of-way.

torquin' it up with

DOUGIE FRANKLIN

Lost Licence

Hi ladies, Dougie Franklin here with some very sad news. I had a little accident and my licence is suspended for a while.

I was caught doing sixty on a sidewalk. I ran through a red light, and also through the post that was holding the red light. And I had locked bumpers with a few other cars. Nine cars. Nobody was hurt. The cars were parked. They were parked in a line at a BMW dealership. I ran over nine BMWs. Luckily the only damage to the truck was from a sunroof jammed under the oil pan. I was insured.

Of course they won't insure me now, but they paid for everything. The insurance agent came right down. So did the adjuster. In fact, lots of people dropped by to see with their own eyes. Great publicity for me so I can't complain. Accidents happen. The important thing is that I've learned a lot. Like I've learned that poles don't just hold up traffic lights, they hold up streetlights and power transformers and power cables that can supply half of the downtown core. I've learned bus shelters make a popping sound as they explode. Stuff like that.

QUICK Driving Tip

Keep your fingers wrapped around the steering wheel—your nose is not an entertainment centre.

CAR GAMES

Nothing spoils a vacation faster than kids constantly whining, "Are we there yet?", "I'm hungry. I'm bored. I think we're lost. This road stinks." Or how about all five of your youngsters chanting, "We want to stop for ice cream!" in the middle of your airline flight to Disneyland?

To make the family trip less of a screaming and pouting festival, here are some games to amuse the kids while you drive. Or if your kids are old enough to drive, here are some games to calm your nerves:

"WORD SCRAMBLE"
or
"DOWR MARBLECS"

Hey kids, try and unscramble the following everyday words. For example the first one, **UPSHUT** is really **SHUTUP.** Enjoy.

UPSHUT	**SINLEEC**	**UVIRRR**
BOWKRPP	**TEOFMTN**	**QQIFNN2E**
TRVU	**ZOZ**	**LELALILOLU**
CORLWOKWZEE	**PRENT**	**FNURB**

WASN'T THAT FUN?

Now try unscrambling these common phrases used in everyday conversation:

SPLEW RRS MUBS PLUNT GNURINGLY
YABBA DABBA DOO!
US DEFT GRILL UBU SNO TIDDUS POOTY
SHE SMELL SEA SCHELL BY DEE SEECHORE.
KLAATU BARADA NICTO.
YUU STIPUD DOGDANT *&%!#$+#^?@!
I MA TON A NGURIELDMMGINNEGS CQOUISTNT' TURB-PELT GNU.
QUNADO OMNI FLUNKUS MORITATI.
AH! AH! AH! AH! AH! . . . . WELBOT
DOMO ARIGOTTO "MISTER ROBOTO."
IXNAY, IT'SAY EETHAY OPSCAY!

CAR BINGO

Hey Kids! It's Car Bingo! Next time your family is on a long drive, each of you ask for one of these Car Bingo cards. If you need extras, nag your parents to buy more copies of this book.

To play Car Bingo, just look out the windows at the passing scenery, keeping an eye peeled for the things on your Bingo card. If one of the squares on your card is "GREEN CAR" and you see a green car, you can check off that square. Check off five in a row in any direction, and you win!

(Parents: These puzzles are set up so that the first few squares are easy to find, which will get your kids playing. The rest of the squares are impossible, so you can drive to the moon and back in relative peace.)

BLUE CAR	RED CAR	A STREET	STREET CRIME	A CLEAN STREET
WHITE CAR	A TREE	RADAR TRAP	ROAD SIDE TRASH	ROAD SIDE PARK
A VAN	UGLY SIGNS	FREE TAURUS WAGON	SISKEL & EBERT	NON-SEXIST ADVERTISING
PINE TREE	PINE TREE WITH LEAVES	THE YETI!	TRUCK DRIVER NODDING OFF	A BANK THAT CARES
A LIVE KANG-AROO	ELVIS	LADA THAT RUNS	FAR SIDE OF THE SUN	FAMILY THAT LOOKS HAPPY

Bingo card 1

BETTER CAR THAN OURS	RUDE AD FOR JEANS	A NEW WAY TO ANNOY DAD	A NEW WAY TO BUG MY SISTER	SHEEP
GAR-FIELD CAT ON WINDOW	BAD OUT OF PROV. DRIVER	ONE SHOE IN THE DITCH	ROYAL FAMILY MEMBER NAKED	FORD CAMARO
TRAFFIC JAM	OMAHA	**FREE** THIS PAGE!	LITTER FROM LORENA BOBBIT	CAR ON FIRE
ORANGE ROAD CREW CONES	LIZ TAYLOR EX-HUBBY	ZEBRA	PRINCE EDWARD ISLAND	SHARP LOOKING TRACK PANTS
WORKER LEANING ON SHOVEL	WORKER LEANING ON RAKE	WORKER LEANING ON HAMMER	WORKER LEANING ON YOUR CAR	WORKER WORKING

Bingo card 2

BACK OF MOM'S HEAD	DAD'S BALD SPOT	SLEAZY MOTEL	GREASY HAIRED HITCH-HIKER	HONEST TOW TRUCK DRIVER
UNSAFE LOOKING TRUCK	SCHOOL BUS	STOP SIGN	SPEED LIMIT SIGN	A CAR DOING SPEED LIMIT
VERY UGLY HOUSE	DEPRES-SED LOOKING TEENS	**FREE** ROAD KILL	MOTOR CYCLE DRIVEN SAFELY	NICE MOTEL
ROAD HOG	DRIVER GIVING DAD THE FINGER	NON-SEXIST RAP SONG	SALT FREE SNACK FOOD	CASINO WITH NICE DECOR
COWS	COP EATING DONUT	GOOD SERVICE	UN-SPOILED VIEW	CLEAN REST ROOMS

Bingo card 3

THE CAR BUFFS ABOUT CANADIAN ROADS

HAROLD ASKS:

HAROLD

Our Car Buffs are Uncle Red and local mechanic Dougie Franklin. A reader from California writes, "Dear Car Buffs, we are thinking about vacationing in Canada this year. Are there different driving rules in Canada?"

RED

No, I don't think so. You're from the States, Dougie. It's the same as here, isn't it?

DOUGIE

Are you kidding, Red? Everything is different up here. Like the highway speed limit is 100 miles per hour. Man, I love that.

HAROLD

Uh, Mr. Franklin, that's 100 kilometres per hour.

DOUGIE

Kilometres?

RED

Yeah. Look at the speed limit signs. It says 100 K M per H. Kilometres per hour.

DOUGIE

I thought K M H meant Kanadian Miles per hour.

HAROLD

"Canada" is spelled with a C.

DOUGIE

I thought the K was the French spelling. I mean, half the signs in this country are in two languages. Okay, maybe the speed limit's the same, but in the United States, the left hand lane is the passing lane. Not here.

RED

Yes it is.

DOUGIE

Then why are all the slow drivers always in the left lane?

RED

Well, maybe it just seems that way because you're going a hundred miles an hour.

DOUGIE

I dunno. And another difference is in Canada, the cars don't have horns or turn signals.

HAROLD

Oh yes they do, Mr. Franklin.

DOUGIE

Well, see now that's a waste of money. You're paying for your horn and your turn signals, so why wouldn't you use 'em? Why would anybody buy something and then not use it? That's dumb. When I buy something I use it.

RED

You ever buy a laxative, Dougie?

DOUGIE

No, sir.

HAROLD

Didn't think so.

ANOTHER Cheap Trick
BY DALTON HUMPHREY

Foregoing small items is a big money saver. Not just coffee-cup holders and cigarette lighters, but back seats and floors. What do you need floors for? You're sitting, your feet are on the pedals! Windshield wipers? The roads aren't safe in the rain anyway. When it rains, stay home.

Headlights? Driving at night is dangerous. Stay home.

Turn indicators? Rear view mirror? Side mirrors? If you have to be aware of other drivers, the roads are probably too crowded. Stay home.

Now, if you follow my advice you'll only drive in clear, sunny weather when the roads are empty. That means you'll never get into accidents. So you won't need anti-lock brakes, side impact beams, airbags, and seat belts. Those are only there for accidents. So is insurance right? No insurance, another big saving.

Here's another plus—if you drive only when roads are empty, you won't need a muffler.

BUILD YOUR OWN CAR TANK

There is nothing more embarrassing than getting your car stuck in a ditch somewhere. Well there is one thing more embarrassing, but usually you can count on your wife not to blab.

Anyway I've decided to show you how you can make your car less vulnerable to sink holes, mud slides, avalanches, and quicksand—for those of you who don't have a paved driveway.

SNOW FENCE

To go where angels fear to tread, you need one hell of a tread. A tank tread. This idea is so simple you'll wonder why you didn't think of it. Just turn your car into a tank.

Okay, you're going to need a roll of snow fence, a pair of snips, golf clubs and an axe.

The first step is to disconnect the emergency brake from the left side of your vehicle. That's what the snips are for. If you're not sure which cable it is, cut them all. Who cares about safety? You're building a tank.

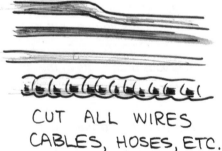

CUT ALL WIRES CABLES, HOSES, ETC.

Now the emergency brake will only stop the right side wheels. To balance that out disconnect your regular brake lines from the right side of the car so they only stop the left side wheels. Just take a 7/16ths wrench and disconnect them at the wheel cylinders. If they're rusted on, just keep kicking until something breaks. (Toes don't need a cast anyway)

Now in order for our tank treads to have room to move freely around the wheels, you have to remove the front half of the front fender and the rear half of the rear fender which you can do easily with a chainsaw.

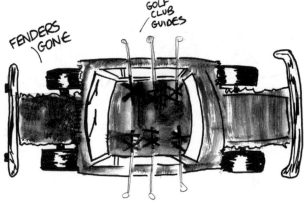

CAR TANK: JUST ADD TREADS

(WARNING: Don't use your own chainsaw)

Now you're ready for your tank tread which you can buy through an army surplus magazine, or you can make yourself from an old escalator, or if you're not made of money, just use a piece of snow fence. It's twice as wide as you need so just cut her in half and you'll have a track for each side of your vehicle.

Mount the golf clubs on the roof with the Handyman's Secret Weapon—duct tape. These will work as guides to keep the treads in line with the wheels. Have the handles attached to the roof so the heads are out to the sides. For long trips, use your driver and for short runs, a putter sounds appropriate.

Now you're ready to roll and when you want to turn left you step on the brake. When you want to turn right you pull on the emergency. And you can go anywhere. From now on you don't need a map of where you're going, just the coordinates.

Remember if the women don't find you handsome, they should at least find you handy.

HAROLD ASKS:

THE CAR BUFFS ABOUT CARS THAT ARE TOO WRECKED TO FIX

HAROLD

*Our Car Buffs are Uncle Red, and Dalton Humphrey, and our letter asks, "Dear Buffs, My car is a complete wreck and I don't feel safe driving it. **What do you do with a car that's too wrecked to fix?"***

DALTON

Well, obviously you should sell the pig.

HAROLD

That's a little unethical, isn't it? Selling a car that's unsafe and worthless?

RED

Well you wouldn't sell it to anyone you know. Would you, Dalton?

DALTON

I would. Don't get me wrong. Friends and neighbours are a treasured and wonderful part of my life. I truly value all of them and I'm blessed to have so many but hey, a buck's a buck.

RED

I think what Dalton is saying Harold is Caveat Emptor, which I believe was the name of the first Roman Used Car Lot.

DALTON

Absolutely. Besides if you sell a friend a bad car and they end up suing you or calling you foul names, or threatening to run over your pet, well, you'll know that this person was never a real friend in the first place.

RED

I think the wording of the ad is the important part. You've gotta say things like "For Sale: as is, where is, stops and goes, mostly stops." Or "Car for Sale: Perfect for people who hate travelling."

DALTON

Well, that's the thing. It's not lying, it's salesmanship. If the car's floor is rusted through, say it's got a classic interior.

RED

Classic?

DALTON

Yeah. Like the Flintstones' car. Don't tell them the car breaks down a lot, just say it's a great way to meet tow truck drivers. If they ask you how the car is on oil, just say "Loves it. Can't get enough of the stuff." It's not lying.

RED

It's salesmanship.

HAROLD

It's perjury.

DALTON

Well, now wait a minute Harold, didn't I hear you trying to get a date with that counsellor from the Girl Guide camp? How did you describe yourself again?

HAROLD

Well, I guess I might have said something along the lines of tall, dark and handsome.

RED

Rather than tall, dork and useless. Sounds about as honest as our car sales pitch.

HAROLD

Not really. The girl didn't break down.

DALTON

Well then, maybe you should be looking at something with a few more miles on her.

 (fig. a)    (fig. b)

Everyone I know would love to own a stretched Cadillac limousine. But no one I know can afford one. It's not the stretch part they can't afford. It's not the limousine part. It's the Cadillac part.

Brand new Cadillacs are expensive. And since no one around here has that kind of money, or even that kind of credit rating, there aren't even any used ones around.

So I'd given up the idea of ever owning a stretched limousine, and was prepared to live with a sagging Possum Van when I had a thought. What if you ignore the "Cadillac" part of stretched Cadillac limousine? And instead substitute the name of a less costly vehicle that might be more available to someone with, say, two hundred bucks to spend.

Start with something more in my price range, like a Volkswagen. (fig. a)

And make a stretched Volkswagen limousine. (fig. b)

Or take a bunch of old vans (fig. c)  (fig. c)

Cut the rusty parts off, like cutting the bruises off an apple, and take the good parts and weld yourself a stretched van limousine. (fig. d)

 (fig. d)

And there's lots of folks around here who'd be glad to get rid of that K-Car in the driveway. (fig. e)

Especially if they knew it was going to a good cause like a stretched K-Car limousine. (fig. f)

 (fig. e)

In fact, since we're breaking the Cadillac tradition in stretched Cadillac limousine, why not break another tradition? Why always stretch it front-to-back?

(fig. f)

Who says that's so great—having a bowling alley on wheels? It just makes the vehicle hard to park. The kids can really misbehave and you can't get at 'em. And like you, it'll eventually sag in the middle.

(fig. g)

So why not stretch it side-to-side? (fig. g & fig. h)

It's just like one of those Humvee things that are all the rage in Hollywood.

(fig. h)

Lots of room to spread out and sleep. And you don't have to worry about people passing you, 'cause you're blocking both lanes.

Think about it. I did.

THE SEVEN STAGES OF PARKING

I'd like to talk to all of you men about what we're all looking for as we drive down the highway of life. A decent place to park. In fact, I see life as the Seven Stages of Parking.

STAGE ONE—You're a kid. All you have to park is your butt. **STAGE TWO**—You're a teenager and you park with a girl who has a good chance of being your future wife. **STAGE THREE**—You're married with kids and you're parking a mini-van at the McDonald's with the Play Area. **STAGE FOUR**—The kids are grown and working at McDonald's, you've got a sports car and are caught parking with a girl who has no chance of being your future wife. This leads immediately to **STAGE FIVE**—You're parking in the garage for a while, where you're also living. **STAGE SIX**—You're old, no car, no licence, no parking spot. **STAGE SEVEN**—You're parked. Permanently. In your own space. Even has your name over it.

Possum Lodge Traffic Bylaws:

#3. Lodge Members may not
    clean, vacuum, or wash
    their cars on Lodge
    Property. (So far
    everyone's been great
    about this bylaw)

    Obey these Bylaws—
or face my frown. I'M SERIOUS!
    Officer Noel Christmas

Don't cut me off—that's my wife's job.

HANDYMAN CORNER

BUILD YOUR OWN FIRETRUCK CAR

Maybe you've always wanted to be in the Volunteer Fire Department, but have never joined because you don't have time or you can't pass the physical or you just don't want to be spending your weekends with the kinds of losers that are attracted to that kind of hobby.

Well, here's a better way. Instead of turning normal citizens into firefighters, why don't we just turn a normal car into a firetruck? Who hasn't thrilled to the sight of a huge firetruck racing past them, roaring down the street to put out a blaze you started totally by accident? It wasn't your fault, it's the lousy instructions that come with electrical appliances.

Okay, first a firetruck needs shovels and picks, and axes. Firetrucks carry these tools on the outside, where firefighters can get 'em in an emergency, like say, a fire. So just drill holes in your trunk lid, slightly larger than the diameter of the handles. Then the tools will sit right in there, ready for use. Don't worry about the damage, because you're going to paint this baby fire engine red.

Now firetrucks have lots of flashing lights. And so do you. Christmas lights. You probably have a set hanging off your eavestrough that you forgot to take down, right? Just hook them to an extension cord. (That will limit the range of your firetruck but any fire that's farther away than the length of an extension cord is probably none of your business.) Attach the bulbs to your firetruck with wire staples, plastic clips, or the Handyman's Secret Weapon—duct tape.

A firetruck also needs a siren. Your horn is a good start, but for extra noise, loosen your alternator belt and your fan belt and your power steering belt just a bit and then, when you start her up, folks will hear you coming. If you really want to be safe, punch a few holes in the muffler.

Now a firetruck needs plenty of hose, so get yourself a number of hoses and reels from the hardware store or you know, borrow them from someone who's not around. Just attach them near the front of the car, so you can hook the hoses right to the engine's water pump, and this becomes a pumper truck. And don't worry about them not matching—we're going to paint this baby fire engine red.

HOOK + LADDER TRUCK *SEDAN*

A firetruck wouldn't be a firetruck without a fire ladder that can turn in any direction. (Fires can happen in any direction and you may park in any direction.) For that you need a rotating platform. Hold a 3-by-3 square of plywood in the middle of your roof and drive a 6-inch spike down through the middle of it. (Make sure no one is in the car when you do this.)

Run a rod through the ends of the ladders and through a couple of screw eyes in the roof to make your pivot point and then run rope up through some pulleys attached to the middle of each unit, and you'll have a ladder that fights fires in two separate directions at the exact same time. And she goes up or down, just like the professional units but at a fraction of the cost.

Just a word of caution: don't drive with the ladders in the straight up position. Personal experience has shown that the ladders will make contact with high tension wires and, although wood doesn't conduct electricity, it burns well. My firetruck unfortunately burned to the ground. Didn't bother me because, as soon as it cools off, I'll be painting it a beautiful fire engine red.

Remember, if the women don't find you handsome, they should at least find you handy.

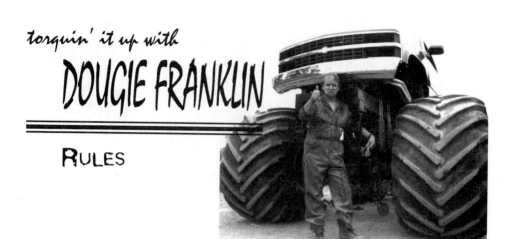

torquin' it up with

DOUGIE FRANKLIN

RULES

Hi ladies, Dougie Franklin here with my monster truck. As you know, this truck was designed to crush cars, so it has to be big. It's a sport. Just like baseball or tennis or demolition derbies. It's the thrill of competition. Of seeing how many cars you can trash. It's very now. And this is not just a bunch of lunatics tearing around a shopping mall parking lot flattening family sedans. We can't get insurance for that. Besides a lot of people leave their pets in the cars and we can't charge admission.

So we have a set of rules that were drawn up by the International Truck and Tractor Association and mostly by the fire department and the stadium owners. Then these rules were printed up and distributed to everyone involved. I always carry a copy with me. "Rule One: Everyone has to wear a helmet." That means drivers, mechanics, officials, people in the grandstands, TV crews and people watching at home. "Rule Two: Don't run over the people in the audience." And then the final rule, which is related to the explosive fuels we use, "Rule Three: No driving around inside old barns." There's a story behind that rule.

And I'll tell you, the people involved in this sport are the finest human beings I've ever met. And their trucks are even better.

QUICK Driving Tip

Feeling bad about your driving record? Remember, even race car drivers crash every month or two. And they're all driving in the same direction!

OLD MAN SEDGWICK'S JUMBO CROSSWORD

Hey kids, here's a puzzle that will really soak up the hours.
It's a crossword puzzle by Old Man Sedgwick. He thought up
all the clues by himself.

ACROSS

1. My Dad's name.
5. The thing I found in my shoe yesterday.
9. How I feel about boats.
13. What Dad always did after a heavy meal.
18. Dad's idea of a heavy meal.
21. Place I bought my shoes.
22. A shoe store I don't frequent much.
23. Mom's maiden name.
24. Too many hats.
25. On my neck.
26. What I do after lunch.
28. First girl I ever kissed.
31. Where I kissed her.
33. Those people I know.
34. Why I hate cheese.
35. Friday, after lunch.
36. Something I find disgusting. (Abbr.)
38. This woke me up once.
39. I can sleep through this just fine.
42. Something my sister finds disgusting. (Plural)
43. The thing they found in my locker that got me fired from the meat packing plant in 1948.
44. Where I found that thing.
45. An animal.
46. A colour I don't much care for.
47. The first number of my locker combination.
50. My best shoes are ___.
51. Somewhere I've never been but always wanted to go.
52. The other place I'd love to go even more than that one.
55. The year I rode a Zeppelin.
56. A tasty food to some.
58. What I told Diefenbaker.
66. Last week I was ____.
67. A book I like.
68. That other book.
69. The one I read before that.
70. My doctor told me "You have to cut back on all ____."
71. See 65 down.
73. The part that broke on my snowblower.
75. The part I thought broke.
77. The other part I thought it might be that broke.
78. My favourite TV show.
79. The star of the show.
80. The other guy I always thought would make a good guest on the show.
82. I heard a kid say this yesterday. (Slang)
83. Last night I felt _____ .
85. My least favourite TV show.
86. A show I don't mind all that much.
87. Hiding place.

DOWN

1. My cousin's old dog.
2. The thing I never used.
3. The thing I used instead.
4. Where I lost my hat once.
6. I had _____ stuck in my ear once.
7. So did my friend _____.
9. But not his brother _____.
11. I just opened a book to page _____.
13. Bathroom need.
14. Bedroom need.
16. Kitchen need.
18. What Mom called Dad once during an argument.
21. I am not allergic to this.
22. This either.
25. If I were a girl I'd _____.
27. My #1 concern.
28. Where I left my gloves when I sat down to do this crossword thingee.
30. I can't eat this.
31. I know a dentist who drives a _____

33. Last name of the guy on channel 8 right now.
34. What he's wearing.
36. I never bought one of these.
38. My _____ hurts a bit.
39. If I had a dog, I bet I'd name him _____.
40. Or maybe _____. After all, whoever heard of a dog with that name?
41. A guy who might have heard of a dog with that name, now that I think about it.
44. I rented one of these once.
46. I didn't get that joke about _____.

53. Thursday.
56. A funny thing.
58. Another funny thing.
59. Two more funny things. (Plural)
61. Something that someone should invent to make life easier.
62. A guy who would never invent 61 down. Not in a million years.
65. See 71 across.
67. I never tried this. (Latin)
75. Same as 31 down, but smaller.
82. One word I don't understand.
83. Some jumbled letters.

QUICK Driving Tip

Hate tailgaters? Try wiring a push button on your dashboard that turns on your brake lights. Gets 'em every time.

THE SELF-CLEANING CAR

Here's an easy way to build an automatic, self-contained, mobile washer that keeps your car continuously clean. Just like going to the car wash except it's free and you don't have to go the car wash.

Now for the sprinklers, you'll need a whole bunch of sprinklers. It's that simple. You'll find sprinklers on people's front lawns long after they've gone to bed.

Mount them all over the car using bolts, rivets, or if you work for the government you may have the time to sit and magnetize them. But if you like the chrome look, use the Handyman's Secret Weapon—duct tape.

Attach all the sprinklers together using garden hoses from the same

YOUR RAD IS FULL ~~HALF FULL~~ HAS SOME WATER IN IT.

source mentioned above. Now you need a source of water—one that moves with the car, so you can wash your vehicle on the move. And you have a source right inside the engine compartment. Namely the water pump and the radiator. All you have to do is tap into them.

Don't forget that being a mobile car wash, it does not have an unlimited supply of water, so what you're going to have to do is recycle your water. (I don't mean the way people adrift at sea recycle their water.) Measure the exact outside circumference of your car, and get exactly that much eavestroughing. Attach the eavestroughs all the way around the car to catch any runoff. Run a hose from the intake side of the water pump, into the eavestroughs to put the wash water back into the radiator, creating a completely closed system—except, of course, for evaporation. Which you can compensate for by leaving your car out in the rain.

Remember, if the women don't find you handsome, they should at least find you handy.

A WORD
FOR THE YOUNG DRIVERS

I know that we have a lot of young people out there reading this as some sort of a punishment and I know Harold gets a chance to talk to you, but that's more of a contractual thing that he insisted on, rather than a point of view that has any real value to it. Now to my mind you need someone a little older who's been down the road a time or two to give you a little advice on growing up.

Maybe you've just gotten your driver's licence and you're excited as heck about that and the next thing you know you've stolen a car. And naturally you go over to your high school to do a little showing off. Doing donuts and figure eights in the flower beds, up on two wheels and then in through the front doors so you can peel rubber up and down the halls.

I know that may sound like a lot of fun, but please, play it smart: wear your seatbelt.

QUICK Driving Tip

Side impact beams save lives. They also cost money. Instead, park at the side of a highway, right against a guard rail and jack your car up like you're changing a tire. Whip out an acetylene torch, weld a section of guard rail to the side of your car. Cut it off the support posts, and drive away with a safer vehicle. Repeat on the other side. (Avoid welding your doors shut and don't drive off until you've completely cut off the piece of guard rail.)

ONTARIO
POSSUM
KEEP 'EM

Stay back. Blind driver.

HAROLD ASKS:

THE CAR BUFFS ABOUT BOOLEAN LOGIC

HAROLD

Our Car Buffs today are my Uncle Red and his best friend, Dougie Franklin. The question comes from someone who just bought a new car.

DOUGIE

Cars are my specialty.

RED

Golly, there's nothing Dougie here doesn't know about cars.

HAROLD

Excellent. "My new car has electronic ignition and computer-controlled fuel injection. I was wondering what is the importance of Boolean Logic in computer programming?"
Oh yeah, excellent question.

RED

Dougie?

DOUGIE

Yeah?

RED

You wanna field that question?

DOUGIE

Was there a question in there, Red?

HAROLD

Yeah, the importance of Boolean Logic in computers. You know, theorems, logical propositions, and/or gates, set-theory. We just covered it in algebra.

DOUGIE

Uh, oh yeah. Well, that is a good question. But I can't answer that question, because they didn't mention what make of car they bought.

RED

Well, let's just say it was a Ford product. What then?

DOUGIE

Oh, okay, a Ford product. Well, then I would say the importance of Boolean Logic in a Ford is less than in a GM product, but more than a Chrysler product. Basically your domestic Boolean Logic is not as fancy and intricate and convoluted as some of the imported Boolean Logic, and it's much more reliable. So when the set theory breaks down, it's easier to buy new And/Or Gates, or the Or/And Gates, and the And/Or/Maybe Gates. And it costs a lot less to rebuild a domestic theorem than one of those flimsy imported jobs.

RED

So you prefer North American Booleans?

DOUGIE

Oh yeah, and buying North American Booleans keeps the jobs in our country for our mathematicians.

Just say NO to Harold.

STREAMLINING

Nowadays cars have really fancy streamlined bodies. Whereas anything you can afford has a big, boxy, ugly body. (I'll resist the temptation to point out the similarities to your body.)

Of course streamlining isn't new.

We had streamlining back when I was a teenager. In fact racing cars were really streamlined, with lightweight aluminum bodies that looked like this....

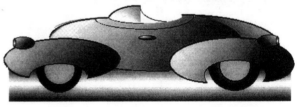

(FIGURE 1)

And this...

(FIGURE 2)

And even this...

(FIGURE 3)

Unfortunately, your car doesn't look like those cars. It's not made of aluminum. It's made of rust. And it looks like this...

(FIGURE 4)

But now you can have an aluminum streamlined racy-looking car. All you need is to take that 14 foot aluminum boat you accidently drove over the rocks last summer...

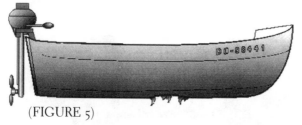

(FIGURE 5)

Then remove all the metal body parts from your car...

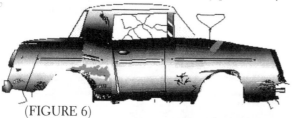

(FIGURE 6)

Don't discard this, because I'm sure you'll think of some great project you can use it for, like a spare bedroom or a walk-in closet. Now take the boat, and remove the outboard motor, again saving it because you might be able to use it someday for something, or who knows, the guy who owns it may figure out that you took it and he'll want it back.

Now, turn the boat over, and mount it on the car frame like this.

(FIGURE 7)

Add paddles at the back for fins, and there you go. Your very own Puntiac. Or an Oldsmoboat.

Now I actually took this a bit further, because when I removed some of the body panels, the engine fell out. So I took the outboard motor, mounted it on the back like this...

(FIGURE 8)

Then duct taped it in place, removed the prop and turned it into a hood ornament, and attached paddles to the propellor shaft of the motor.

This car is now my biggest fan. I started her up and what do you know...

(FIGURE 9)

I got 100 dollars for it from the scrap metal dealer.

MAKE YOUR CAR GO FASTER

It doesn't take magic to make your car go faster. It takes logic and perse-
verance which, at the Lodge, is much rarer than magic. So take a few
minutes to understand the principles of friction, gravity, and the internal
combustion engine. The solution is found with physics, not with psychics.

THE IMPORTANCE OF HORSEPOWER

Horsepower is the term for the size of the guns your motor can deliver. It's
determined by three things—the size of the engine (displacement), the
tightness of the engine (compression) and the explosiveness of the fuel
(where are my eyebrows?).

- Start with the biggest engine you can find. Big things have big
  engines. ie. semis, earth movers, trains, cruise ships. Get one of
  those engines and put it into your K-car.

- Increase the compression by tightening the head bolts with a
  crescent wrench welded to the end of a flagpole for extra torque.
  Wrap the whole engine in duct tape. Use two layers in opposite
  directions for the tightest seal since Marineworld put vodka in the
  performance pool.

- Now you want a really explosive gas. I suggest jet or rocket fuel or
  anything with the numbers 238 after it. Increasing the spark also
  helps. Try getting a power transformer from a nearby pole when
  the power is off (that's important). Wire the transformer between
  the ignition coil and the distributor. It will raise the voltage from
  50,000 to 125,000,000,000,000,000,000,000,000,
  000,000,000,000,000,000,000,000,000,000,000,000,000 volts
  which will make the car easier to start and give you a more
  interesting hairstyle.

There are ways to get even more horsepower, but I feel they're just
too dangerous.

REDUCING FRICTION

While friction is often a good thing and a key component in the
propagation of the human race, it is a bad thing in every other race. There
are two ways to reduce friction in your car. One is to have a well-made car
that uses only the best materials under strict tolerances with stringent

quality control and the other, which actually happens around here, is to really lay on the lubricant. (See also Propagation) A good rule to live by is, "If it's dry, something is wrong" (with the exception of the driver's seat). Cover everything with lubricant—the shocks, the springs, the linkage, the engine, the driveshaft, the tires, the hood, the windshield, the air freshener, the steering wheel, the door handles, but not the cigarette lighter. A cigarette lighter popping out of your hand can bring an unwanted understanding of the term "grease fire."

DEALING WITH GRAVITY

It's really difficult to reduce gravity. Even in the deepest valley there is still enough gravity to get a person down and keep him there. So you're better off to get gravity working for you. When you're climbing a hill, you're fighting gravity so don't try to go fast. Why waste the gas? Just go ten or fifteen miles over the speed limit.

But when you come over the crest of the hill and start heading down, well that, my friend, is a different story. Lay the coals to her. Put both feet on the accelerator and wind her right out. As long as you can focus with either eye, you're not going the maximum. Einstein says that as you approach the speed of light, time will slow down. So if you're running late, you'll make up time. Einstein also said when you get moving fast enough, distances shrink. So you can squeeze your car in between two trucks.

Unfortunately Einstein proved that there are problems as you reach the speed of light because you will have infinite mass. Which unfortunately can cut into the mileage. But you'll probably notice that around the twelve-hundred-pound mark you have no neck and your gut starts honking the horn. That would be a good time to ease off on the gas pedal. And don't worry about the cops. Radar guns can't register the speeds you'll be hitting and most policemen are hesitant to flag down any vehicle coming towards them at over 500 miles per hour. Especially if you've just dropped the cigarette lighter.

The most important element is common sense. There's no point in going really, really fast if there are other cars or pedestrians or farm animals in the vicinity. Driving fast can be fun and safe, but not if you do it. Driving fast is for normal people. The fact that you're reading this book disqualifies you.

QUICK Driving Tip

If your facial skin is making you deaf, you're driving too fast.

HAROLD'S
RADIATOR CROSSWORD

Here's a crossword puzzle I made up about your car's cooling system.

	1	**2**	**3**	**4**	**5**	**6**	**7**	**8**	**9**
10									
11									
12									
13									

ACROSS
1. Plural of radiator.
10. The fluid in the radiator that doesn't freeze.
11. A hose made of rubber.
12. The device that measures your radiator's temperature.
13. A fancy word for rust that's spelled a lot like corruption .

DOWN
1. The Royal Navy Universal Horse Cavalry. (Initials)
2. Acronym for Austin Texas Bureau of Economic Overseeing.
3. What the word "timber" might sound like if your lips were frozen.
4. Acronym for International Fire Extinguisher Manufacturers Rodeo.
5. The sound guys make when they're whooping it up.
6. Acronym for Tennessee Extra-terrestrial Hospitality Suite Supervisor.
7. Short form for Ontario Energy Office Terminal Imploders.
8. Acronym for Registered Zipheads Society, Alberta Office.
9. How a really bad speller might write the word "Seating."
10. Stuff you hang on your wall.

See? Wasn't that fun?

Try making up your own crossword puzzle. Although if you want my advice, you won't choose all the Across words before you choose any of the Down words.

SAYING GOODBYE TO YOUR FAVOURITE CAR

No matter how much we do, there comes a time in the life of any car when we have to say goodbye. This can be upsetting and even traumatic for the owner, particularly if he still has two more years of car payments. Here are a few procedural steps you can take to ensure closure at this time of great emotional stress.

- Remove everything from the car that has any personal significance for you—the paper cups, the cigarette butts, the spent shells, your underwear, your passenger's underwear, the previous owner's underwear, the fuzzy dice, the dingle balls, the sex lights, the 8 tracks, the Garfield window sticker, the pizza boxes, the pizza.
- Leave anything that you never used—maps, napkins, air freshener, emergency brake, turn signals, owner's manual, rear view mirror, seat belts.
- Step back from the car and think about significant memories that it holds for you—

  Car Chicken, Car Chase, Car Ceration,

  Drag Race, Drag Net, Drag Queen,

  Prom Night, Promise Night, Prompt Night,

  Flat Tire in the Pouring Rain, Hot Upholstery in the midday Sun,

  Small Errors, Medium Impacts, Big Explosions.
- Say a silent prayer of thanks: "Dear Lord, Thank you for making this car and for making it run and for making the previous owner leave the keys in it outside the 7-11. Thank you for not harming my self or other people with this car. Sorry about the raccoon. Amen."
- Then just turn and walk away. No second thoughts. No looking back. Forget the car. Go to the nearest ATM, take out $50 and buy another one just like it.

THE LAST WORD

I know it may be too late for the truth but I'm gonna give it a try anyway. Take a look at the cars they're making today—safe, fuel efficient, comfortable, reliable, climate controlled with hi-fi, low maintenance, and cheaper than ever when compared to the average wage. Sure they're boring, but as I get older, I'm more receptive to boredom.

Mind you it's still better to give than receive. So stand up wherever you are and raise a glass of whatever you've got, and let's salute the men and women who are designing and building the cars of today, and let's give a little prayer that they don't give all the jobs to robots because, as all Chevy Vega drivers know, it's human error that makes life worth living.

And drive safely. I want you around to buy my next book.

IOIOIOIOIOIOIOIOIOIOIOIOIOIOIOIOIOIOIOIOIOIOIOIOIOIOIO

FREE UPGRADE!!!

For those of you who purchased my first book, The Red Green Book, the following is an upgrade. It works with both DOS and Windows. (Sorry, Mac users.)

The Red Green Book Version 1.1

• In the poem, "Pruning Time," delete the word "cuts" and insert the phrase "bludgeons in twain"

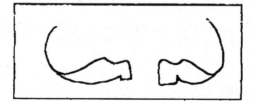

• Cut and paste these shoes onto the feet of the Silver-Tufted Walker

• In "Quality Time—Phase Two" underline the word "vomits".

IOIOIOIOIOIOIOIOIOIOIOIOIOIOIOIOIOIOIOIOIOIOIOIOIOIOIO